# 100 Ideas for Primary Teachers:
# Reading for Pleasure

**Scott Evans**

BLOOMSBURY EDUCATION

LONDON   OXFORD   NEW YORK   NEW DELHI   SYDNEY

BLOOMSBURY EDUCATION

Bloomsbury Publishing Plc

50 Bedford Square, London, WC1B 3DP, UK

29 Earlsfort Terrace, Dublin 2, Ireland

BLOOMSBURY, BLOOMSBURY EDUCATION and the Diana logo are
trademarks of Bloomsbury Publishing Plc

First published in Great Britain 2023 by Bloomsbury Publishing Plc

This edition published in Great Britain 2023 by Bloomsbury Publishing Plc

A catalogue record for this book is available from the British Library

ISBN: PB: 978-1-8019-9190-2; ePDF: 978-1-8019-9189-6;
ePub: 978-1-8019-9187-2

2 4 6 8 10 9 7 5 3 1 (paperback)

Typeset by Newgen KnowledgeWorks Pvt. Ltd., Chennai, India
Printed and bound in the UK by CPI Group Ltd, CR0 4YY

To find out more about our authors and books visit www.bloomsbury.com
and sign up for our newsletters.

# Contents

Acknowledgements        vi
Introduction        viii
How to use this book        xi

**Part 1: Raising reading children**        **1**
1 Children's Choice        2
2 Daily Read        3
3 Recognise All Reading        4
4 Independent Reading        6
5 Readers' Rights        7
6 Reading Surveys        8
7 Time to Talk        9
8 Early Reading Experiences        10
9 Reasons to Read        11
10 Me as a Reader        12
11 Incorporate Interests        13
12 Every Child a Free Reader        14
13 Bibliotherapy Books        15
14 Empathy-Boosting Books        16
15 Re-Read        17

**Part 2: Creating a reading classroom**        **19**
16 Reading Classrooms        20
17 Class Book        21
18 Working Wall        22
19 Classroom Collections        23
20 Currently Reading        24
21 Book Buddies        25
22 Reading Recommendations        26
23 Book of the Week        28
24 Reading Responses        29
25 Reading Roundups        30
26 Reading Scrapbook        31
27 First Chapter Friday        32
28 Sign Out Sheets        33
29 Reading Reflections        34
30 Reading Resolutions        35
31 Reading Route        36

**32** Super Readable Books 37
**33** Reading Role Play 38
**34** Book Match 39
**35** Topic Texts 40

**Part 3: Being a reader teacher** **41**
**36** Reading Aloud 42
**37** Reading By Example 43
**38** Reading Role Models 44
**39** Know Your Books 45
**40** Staffroom Selection 46
**41** Signature Sharing 47
**42** Staff Book Club 48
**43** Reading and Research (R&R) 50
**44** Reading Roundtables 52
**45** Reading Reviews 53
**46** Recent Releases 54
**47** Reading Conferences 55

**Part 4: Leaders are readers** **57**
**48** Reading Lead 58
**49** Head Reader 60
**50** Senior Readership Team 62
**51** Curriculum Reading Champions 63
**52** Put Reading on the Plan! 64
**53** Book Budget 65
**54** Reading Audit 66

**Part 5: Setting up a reading school** **67**
**55** Reading Representatives 68
**56** Reading Assemblies 69
**57** Reading Spine 70
**58** Whole School Books 71
**59** Book-Based Curriculum 72
**60** Reading Representation 73
**61** Book Mapping 74
**62** Reading All Year Round 75
**63** Book Club 76
**64** Residential Reading 77
**65** Books At Breakfast Club 78
**66** Digital Reading 79
**67** Book Awards 80
**68** Rethinking Reading Rewards 82
**69** Reader Recognition 84
**70** Transition Time 85

**Part 6: Understanding text types**    **87**
71 Fantastic Fiction    88
72 Face the Facts    89
73 Poetry for Pleasure    90
74 The Power of Picture Books    91
75 Graphic Novels    92

**Part 7: Cultivating a reading community**    **93**
76 Reading Newsletters    94
77 School Socials    95
78 Reading Volunteers    96
79 Community Collaboration    97
80 Festival Friends    98
81 Book Fair    99
82 Fundraising and Finance    100
83 Festival of Reading    102
84 Drives and Donation Schemes    104

**Part 8: Love your libraries**    **105**
85 School Library    106
86 School Librarian    107
87 Local Library    108
88 Summer Reading Challenge    109

**Part 9: Engaging with your reading
environment**    **111**
89 Door Displays    112
90 Front-Facing    113
91 Make Reading Visible    114
92 Reading Places and Spaces    115

**Part 10: Participating with parents and
families**    **117**
93 Parent Partners    118
94 Parents' Evenings    119
95 Report On Reading    120
96 Reading Workshops    121

**Part 11: Working with writers and
illustrators**    **123**
97 Author of the Month    124
98 Author Visits    126
99 Adopt An Author    128
100 Virtual Visits    129

Appendix: Whole School Books (Idea 58)    130

# Acknowledgements

First and foremost, I have to start by thanking the team at Bloomsbury Education who have helped me so much throughout the publishing process and for welcoming me so warmly to work with them. It's been an absolute pleasure and privilege, and I'm honoured to be published by you. Special thanks to Hannah Marston and Cathy Lear, my ever-patient editors, for their excellent insight, wisdom, assurance and advice along the way.

To all the children I've taught in my classes or had the opportunity to read to, read with, or talk about books with, I want to say thank you for everything I've learned from you in return, and for being the main reason for writing this book. Equally, to all the teachers, teaching assistants, librarians, office and support staff, caretakers, cleaners, cooks, parents, families, schools, authors, illustrators, poets, booksellers, bloggers, organisations and everyone else I've ever worked with in an educational capacity. You change children's lives for the better every day, especially by encouraging them to enjoy reading, and you're all **outstanding** in your own way.

I've also been blessed to have had many brilliant teachers of my own, and heartfelt thanks must go to Mrs (Yvonne) Davies, Mr (James) Kent and Mrs (Elaine) Carter-Evans, who set me on the path from my first steps at primary school to secondary school, and also the University of Winchester and University of South Wales, whose libraries became my second homes when training to become a teacher. As the Manic Street Preachers sing 'libraries gave us power', and that is no more true than that of my local libraries. Extended thanks go to the staff at Cwmbran Library – especially Julia – where I worked, and where I maxed out my special staff library card over its limit with as many children's books as I could borrow to be the reader teacher that I am today.

I feel extremely fortunate to have such an amazing, dedicated, caring and thoughtful family. I will forever owe my achievements to them. My parents, Siân and Martyn. My grandparents, Shirley, George, Kath, and Glyn. My great-grandmother, Mabel. Thank you all for inspiring my love of reading from an early age. I'm eternally grateful for the greatest gifts you've given me including the time and memories we've shared and spent reading together, and the books that you have filled my home, my life, my head and my heart with.

Finally, I'm forever indebted to my girlfriend, Emily, for always being by my side through all my successes and struggles, and without whom this book would never have been written as I wouldn't be where I am without you. You are my strongest supporter and light of my life. From reading first drafts to your endless belief, joy, kindness, love, encouragement and enthusiasm, you've allowed me to grow and flourish in ways I could never have imagined. Ultimately, this is dedicated to you because sharing life with a perfect partner makes everything worthwhile.

# Introduction

Reading is the most important thing we can teach in our schools. This is a bold statement to make, but the role of reading within a child's life has never been greater. Research shows that it's such a powerful factor that it determines a child's future aspirations, irrespective of their parents' level of education or their socio-economic background (OECD, 2002). Reading can improve a child's comprehension, vocabulary, spelling, speaking, listening, writing and overall general knowledge. Not only does it make a big difference to a child's educational achievement across the curriculum, it also affects their personal, social and emotional development. But despite so many positives, there has been a definite decline in children choosing to read.

Therefore, reading for pleasure cannot be left to happen by chance. With schools now under pressure to teach a congested curriculum and achieve results – and families pushed for time or lacking the required literary skills, knowledge or confidence to pass on the pleasure of reading to their children – it is happening less. Compounded by the consequences of libraries closing, school and household budgets becoming tighter and electronic devices turning into the entertainment of choice, as well as the effects of the global pandemic, there seems little opportunity for children to develop a lifelong love of reading that could benefit them in so many ways. As teachers, we must actively invest and involve ourselves in the reading for pleasure process, seeing it as something beyond what children do in the classroom and equipping ourselves with a multitude of methods at our disposal to revitalise reading with a real rapture and reverence in order to keep children reading throughout their lives.

Combining clear practical advice, activities, ideas and inspiration, together with real tried and tested classroom-based experiences, *100 Ideas for Primary Teachers: Reading for Pleasure* will give teachers the tools, tips and techniques they need to create and sustain a positive reading culture where, as a result, children leave school not just having learned how to read, but wanting to read.

The ideas in the book are based on the 'Reading Roadmap', my five-point framework to revolutionise reading in schools. Each step in the focused framework not only influences the following – from the 'reading child' out to the 'reading community', but also the reverse – from the 'reading community' into the 'reading child'. By creating a classroom reading culture for children, being reader teachers and reader leaders, striving to become a reading school and cultivating a reading community, teachers can raise children who are able, active, avid and accomplished readers.

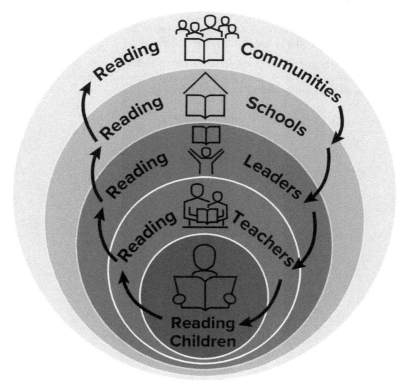

Reading Roadmap

To support teachers on this journey, there will be ideas included on one-off lessons or activities; lessons or parts of lessons that can be woven into your teaching sequences; pedagogical and practical activities to develop reading for pleasure in the classroom and across the school; ways in which teachers and leaders can be readers; how to use the school and local libraries more effectively; engage parents and families in reading; and collaborate with writers and illustrators.

Whether you are training to teach, an early career teacher, an experienced teacher, a middle, senior or subject leader, someone who loves or loathes teaching reading, or even a school librarian or university lecturer, this book will have something for you. Some of these suggestions might be new to you, some might already be in place in your school, and some may be a little radical in their approach.

Remember that reading for pleasure isn't rocket science but neither is it a once-a-week lesson, an off-the-shelf remedy, or an overnight success; and no child, class, teacher, or school is the same, so some of these ideas will work better within your setting than others.

If you have any questions, want to know more about an idea, or would like to share what you're doing with reading, please feel free to get in touch by tweeting me **@MrEPrimary** on Twitter.

# How to use this book

This book includes quick, easy and practical ideas for you to dip in and out of to help you deliver effective and engaging maths lessons.

Each idea includes:

- a catchy title, easy to refer to and share with your colleagues
- an interesting quote linked to the idea
- a summary of the idea in bold, making it easy to flick through the book and identify an idea you want to use at a glance
- a step-by-step guide to implementing the idea.

Each idea also includes one or more of the following:

### Teaching tip

Practical tips and advice for how and how not to run the activity or put the idea into practice.

### Taking it further

Ideas and advice for how to extend the idea or develop it further.

### Bonus idea ★

**There are 57 bonus ideas in this book that are extra-exciting, extra-original and extra-interesting.**

Share how you use these ideas and find out what other practitioners have done using #100Ideas. There are other, idea-specific hashtags listed throughout the book as well.

# Raising reading children

Part 1

# Children's Choice

"Everyone feels included when we choose our class book. It's so exciting to see who wins!"

**Asking children to vote for their class book offers them opportunities to take ownership of what they want to read, become respectful readers by exercising their reading rights, and understand some simple aspects of decision-making and democracy in action, through their choice and voice.**

**Teaching tip**

Use mathematical resources and graphing tools to discuss the data and record the results.

**Taking it further**

Wrap up nominated books to conceal their covers and write the first lines, paragraph, page or blurb on them. This will entice children to consider the content rather than be influenced by the covers.

**Bonus idea** ★

Turn this idea into **#ClassroomChoice** with teaching staff participating too. You could also use it for children to make other reading-related rulings such as selecting your 'Author of the Month' **(Idea 97)**.

#ChildrensChoice

As a child, do you remember teachers reading books to the class? Do you remember voting for that book choice? Your first answer will hopefully be yes, but your second will probably be no. But how transformational would it have been for you to have had the power to pick the class book?

Pupil voice means a whole-school commitment to listening to children. This is no different for reading. Create a choosing culture by setting up a station in your classroom for children to have their say on your class book. Display a range of nominated books, then handle, look at and talk about them before asking children to vote for the one they'd most like to read. Discuss how they can also abstain and how the majority wins.

Make voting systems age-appropriate and inclusive by using a variety of: counters and baskets; named pegs; tally charts; a good old 'hands up'; a head-to-head, knock-out **#BattleOfTheBooks** style tournament; a secretive **#BookBallot**; or online polling technology to increase interaction. Watch out, it can get very competitive!

Return the non-winning books to your classroom collection so children can go and find the book they voted for to read themselves after being so passionate about it.

# Daily Read

"Reading every day is not just enjoyable for everyone; it's the entitlement of every child."

**Lay firm foundations for a lifetime love of reading by doing it daily.**

Routines are commonplace in classrooms because they bring calm and comfort to children's lives. When they are clear, consistent, modelled and secured, these patterns of predictability help children to form healthy habits from an early age, in knowing the expectations and giving them the confidence to complete tasks on their own.

Adding a daily dose of reading into their routines can help children to become regular readers. Sadly, many children are now reading less than ever before or not at all, but you can actively change this. If you haven't already established an everyday reading routine in your classroom, it's not too late.

Look at the structure of your school day. It should go without saying that reading lessons are part of your school's everyday curriculum but think about how you can also timetable opportunities for daily reading aloud of your class book **(Idea 17)** and regular independent reading **(Idea 4)**, depending on what works well for you and your class. Display it on visual timetables so children know when to expect it.

Traditionally, this is done at the end of the day but too often this time gets lost, so use other opportunities like at the beginning of the day, before or after break and lunch time.

**Teaching tip**

Make sure that the time to read every day is not only made but is also protected by you at a classroom level, and your senior leadership and management team at a whole school level to show its importance.

**Taking it further**

Coordinate across the whole school, key stages or year groups to schedule reading at the same time every day for it to become a permanent part of each child's **#ReadingRoutine.**

**#DailyRead**

# Recognise All Reading

"All reading is good reading. Recognising this is empowering, enlightening and essential."

**To give children the most dynamic and deepest reading experiences, we must recognise and respect all reading, so that they not only read widely but read what they want, to find the breakthrough book(s) that help them to love reading for life.**

**Teaching tip**

Recognising all reading not only applies to text types and formats but also to different reading situations. Consider how whole class, guided, independent, 1:1, peer, group, echo, choral and cross-curricular reading can all feature as part of your reading offer.

We currently live in a golden age of children's literature with so many talented writers and illustrators creating outstanding new, inclusive and diverse books.

When we talk about literature, we need to ensure that we provide children with a broad and balanced reading diet of texts of all types such as fiction, non-fiction, poetry, picture books and graphic novels, because access to these options opens other doors, opportunities and ways of reading for them.

Re-evaluate which genres and formats of reading are available in your school.

Do you have different fictional subgenres such as science fiction, historical, fantasy, mystery, funny, myths and more? Are factual books up-to-date, appealing and accessible for children to read both for pleasure and purpose? Do children have access to the classics as well as recent releases? Do you also ensure that there are magazines, newspapers, comics, joke books, sports reports and programmes, song lyrics, cookbooks, maps and encyclopaedias for a mix of reading material? It's equally important to recognise that reading can happen anywhere, such as on the labels of tins and packets, instructions, manuals, posters and advertisements, and to provide these in school for children too.

**#Recognise AllReading**

What about different formats: hardbacks, paperbacks, large print editions, dyslexia-friendly and super readable books, audiobooks and ebooks? Technology now enables us to no longer need to rely on physical copies of a book and to adapt formats to each individual child's specific needs, so maximise its means and potential.

**Taking it further**

Another way of recognising all reading is considering how children can play an active part in the decision making when buying books to have in your school. Regular reading surveys **(Idea 6)** can help to identify children's preferences and track the impact of changes.

# Independent Reading

"Independent reading rightfully puts reading into children's hands, giving them 'me' time."

**Develop children's reading resilience, stamina, self-reliance and patience, as well as encourage them to read at their own pace by including independent reading time.**

**Teaching tip**

Don't police children's choices or deny them the chance to chat about what they're reading during independent reading. Use it as time to talk **(Idea 7)** and make reading recommendations **(Idea 22)**.

**Taking it further**

During independent reading time, you could sit with children and read your own book by example **(Idea 37)**, and talk with them about their book choices and yours.

**Bonus idea** ★

Offer other opportunities to independently read, such as after work has been completed in lessons, during free choice time and at break and lunch times. Help them to reach a state of reading flow with longer independent reading times too.

#Independent Reading

Independent reading is sustained and uninterrupted time when children read on their own, with minimal to no assistance from adults. This time allows them to take ownership of what they want to read and explore their preferences through their choice and voice.

Consider the quantity and quality of your independent reading time. Do children do it regularly and is enough time designated towards it?

Are children also involved in decisions about it? Make it learner-led by asking them for their input on aspects (which can all change from day to day) and implementing them, such as:

- when they would like independent reading time to happen;
- where in the classroom they want to read;
- how they position themselves when reading (sitting, standing, lying, leaning, kneeling);
- whether they read solitarily or socially;
- whether they read internally in their heads or externally out loud to each other;
- the level of noise they wish to read in;
- and any other influencing factors.

Independent reading doesn't need to be silent (although there may be times when children prefer to do so), nor confined to the classroom, or only sitting at seats. Use relaxed reading spaces around your classroom or the school **(Idea 92)**, and consider children's comfort levels when reading.

# Readers' Rights

"Readers' rights not only give children their own voice, but their own choice, in reading."

**Consider children's reading rights, promote their principles and permit them the same reading habits we practise as adults with this insightful idea based on Daniel Pennac's book.**

First published in 1992, *The Rights of the Reader* by Daniel Pennac is a book reflecting his belief that readers have rights: to read what, how, where and when they want, and also NOT to read.

**Teaching tip**

Adapt and apply *The Rights of the Reader* into *The Rights of the Reader Teacher* to reflect on and revisit which reading rights staff members have in your school. These could include: the right to make, and protect, the time to read; the right to read widely; the right to put down a book if it's not working with your class; and more.

Search online to find the rights presented in a printable poster illustrated by Quentin Blake. Share the ten points with the children and discuss them. Do the children feel that they have these reading rights in your class? What could you do as a teacher or class to ensure that these rights are recognised? What would you change? Is there anything you would add? Are these reading rights relevant for your class, or would they like to offer other rights that are more personal to them? More relevant rights could include: the right to Recognise All Reading **(Idea 3)**; the right to read in the language of your choice; the right to 'do the voices' when reading; the right to change your book if you're not enjoying it; the right to see yourself reflected in a book etc.

Ask children to make their own rights of the reader lists to understand more about them and what they value individually as readers. As a class, collect their ideas to create your own manifesto to be displayed to remind everyone of their readers' rights in your class. Children could also design their own illustrated posters showing each point.

**#ReadersRights**

# Reading Surveys

"They are one of the easiest and most efficient methods to learn about our children as readers."

**See a snapshot of how children in your class perceive reading through the lens of a survey.**

Start off the school year by surveying children to gain a good grasp of their attitudes, appreciation and access towards reading. You could also carry out termly 'check-ins' by repeating the surveys to track how reading tastes and thoughts have changed over the year — hopefully for the better!

Questions should be open and closed, require a range of multiple choice or more detailed answers, and be adapted to what you want to learn about the children as readers.

Examples of questions could include:

- What/When/Where/Why/How/How often do you like to read?
- Who is your favourite author/illustrator/poet?
- Do you like to read fiction/non-fiction/poetry/picture books/graphic novels?
- Books I have liked/disliked reading are...
- Are you a member of a local library?
- How do you feel when you read?
- How would you describe yourself as a reader?
- How has your teacher helped or supported your enjoyment of reading this year?
- Tell me three reading facts about yourself.
- Draw a picture that shows something about you as a reader.
- I would read more if...
- If I could read anything I wanted to, I would read...
- If I could change one thing about reading in my classroom/school, it would be...

**Teaching tip**

Complete surveys using technology to record responses at the touch of a button and for easier analysis.

**Taking it further**

Conduct a **#SchoolSurvey** to see the bigger picture, and a **#StaffSurvey** to find out more about their knowledge of children's literature and how confident they feel about applying it in the classroom.

**Bonus idea** ★

Use this as a transition time activity (**Idea 70**) when meeting your new class for the first time. Based on their reading responses, you can put things into place during the first few weeks of September for the year ahead.

**#ReadingSurveys**

# Time to Talk

"Talking together is one of the tools that really enables children to become readers!"

**Reading is sometimes seen as a solitary activity but seize structured and informal opportunities to promote it at all hours of the school day to make it both shared and social.**

Talking about books is equally as important as reading them. Make the time for talking about books sacrosanct, and protect it against the challenges of a busy timetable and a congested curriculum.

'Book talk' is being able to talk about books through two-way observation, opinion, organisation, opposition, openness and offering of thought with others.

Book talk can occur formally or informally and through deliberate discussions or spontaneous stages. These two types of talk should happen each day so that they become a natural part of your classroom conversations.

During structured book talk sessions, carefully and consciously plan time to lead, model and trigger book talk with children when discussing extracts, illustrations or ideas from texts through questioning. Strategies such as sentence stems also allow and encourage children to agree, build on or challenge a peer's perspective, in a safe and shared space.

Through informal interactions, talk together with children about what they are reading and their thoughts about it; what you're reading and your opinion of it; as well as reviews, recommendations, and any other reading-related dialogue.

**Teaching tip**

Create a collaborative book talk display featuring a reading question, allowing space for children to write their answers on sticky notes alongside it and time to discuss their responses. You can change the question regularly and collate their responses and reflections in some form as a record.

**Taking it further**

Chat to children about reading and books, from first thing in the morning to last thing before they leave, including in the corridors, at playtimes and at transitions during the day, such as when waiting in the line for lunch or during a #ReadingRegister when children could answer their name followed by the title of the book they're reading.

**#TimeToTalk**

# Early Reading Experiences

"As soon as children start at our school, they are completely immersed in reading."

**Build a base which children can rely upon for the rest of their reading lives by thinking about their early reading experiences.**

Establishing a love of reading in the early years is very important as children develop more in the first five years than at any other time (hence why these are called the foundation years). We want children to read for pleasure, and that can only happen if children can read. This starts with phonics which should have high priority in your school, especially in Early Years. Most schools follow phonics programmes that split teaching into phases which systematically build on skills and knowledge of previous learning for children to take part in daily sessions. Alongside this, there are many other elements essential to supporting children to read.

Although decodable books are key, there is also a need to expose children to a range of texts to build their love of reading. They can experience reading through stories, rhymes, poems, sounds, patterns and rhythms of speech, intonation of voice, and gestures and facial expressions as they hear and share a favourite book (often repeated over again). Big books, board books, as well as soft and sensory books, that contain different colours, patterns and textures, should all be shared. Use story sacks and props like puppets to enhance elements such as storytelling.

There should also be opportunities for children to experience 'book behaviours', such as page-turning, understanding the left-to-right and top-to-bottom directionality of English text, and recognising the purpose of simple punctuation.

**#EarlyReading Experiences**

# Reasons to Read

"Everyone has different reasons to read, and we should try to find everyone's reason."

**Helping children to recognise their reasons for reading can be an enlightening experience, because it can lead to them finding their breakthrough books and realising that everyone can be a reader.**

The reasons why we read are plentiful and often include to learn, to be entertained, to be inspired, to empathise and to escape. For children, however, these reasons may not be as clear, and they might not know or be able to articulate them. This can sometimes leave children being called 'reluctant readers', 'resistant readers' or 'non-readers'.

Rather than referring to children by these terms, we should start by proactively recognising any root cause of so-called reluctance, resistance or refusal to read.

Revealing these reasons takes significant time and substantial unpicking. Other ideas such as Readers' Rights **(Idea 5)** and Reading Surveys **(Idea 6)** can also provide insight into these.

Share the reasons why you like to read with the children. Then, discuss how reading is different for everybody and ask why it is important to them as individuals, and to write down the reason(s) why they like or dislike reading. Using their responses, create a collaborative classroom or whole school display to showcase your school community's 'Reasons to Read' from children, staff, families and visitors alike.

Ultimately, the vision and the world we want to create in our classrooms and communities is one where everyone is reading their way to a better life. Respecting each others' reasons to read will help to remind everyone of the universal importance of reading.

> **Teaching tip**
>
> Contact authors and illustrators to ask them why they think it's important to read and add their contributions to your 'Reasons to Read' display.

**#ReasonsToRead**

# Me as a Reader

"Understanding each other as readers is important, insightful and inspiring for everyone."

**This one-page profile is a creative, personal way for children to reflect on what they think about themselves as readers and their reading experiences, as well as understand that they're unique.**

There's a wide range in our classrooms and a greater spectrum across our schools, from those who adore reading to those who can't wait for the chance to tell us how much they hate it.

Understanding readers' identities should be at the core of our classrooms because it supports our ability to provide the right book at the right time to the right child, by getting to know each reader's individual preferences, perspectives and practices.

To begin the process of producing their 'Me as a Reader' posters, children should start by brainstorming what they'd like to identify on it. Some ideas might include: their favourite books, series, authors or genres; the different ways they enjoy reading; and any memorable reading experiences they've had such as reading a class book or joining a book club.

As children work on their posters, give them the freedom to design it however they wish and enourage them to think about what makes them unique as a reader. For example, do they have an interest in a specific genre or author? Do they prefer to read in a particular setting or at a certain time of day?

**#MeAsAReader**
**#ReadingIdentities**

Once they are complete, children could display them in their classroom, school library or at home as a reminder of their love of reading. You could create your own 'Me as a Reader' poster too.

# Incorporate Interests

"Showing a serious interest in children will help them to become interested in reading."

**While children are often happy to spend hours playing sports or games, watching TV or listening to music, they don't always show the same enthusiasm for reading. But the hobbies children have can be a personalised, powerful inspiration to get them reading.**

As teachers, it's our job to engage and inspire our children to learn and read for pleasure. One way to do this is to build on and be guided by children's interests. This makes them feel valued as individuals, and attempting to teach without acknowledging these can lead to missed learning opportunities.

Therefore, it's important for us to recognise children's interests outside of the national curriculum and to find books with links to what they personally enjoy because this makes the reading experience more meaningful for them.

Children's passions are diverse, ranging from sport to science, cooking to crafting, fashion to films, gaming to gardening, and music to much more in between. No matter what they are, find books about them because if children see reading as relevant and relatable, they are more likely to develop a love of it.

While you may already know many of your children's interests, taking a closer look can give you some new information. Take time to observe children's interests in the classroom and other places such as on the playground; speak to parents to see what they participate in and outside of school; and run Reading Surveys **(Idea 6)** to gain a direct perspective of children through their own words.

### Teaching tip

Set up 'Reading Request' sheets for children to describe the types of book they'd like to read according to what appeals to them and use this insight to make your book recommendations more bespoke.

### Taking it further

Reading sports reports, programmes, instruction manuals and recipes or learning song lyrics, the names of plants and animals or learning about famous figures and events can all be ways of integrating interests and reading.

**#IncorporateInterests**

# Every Child a Free Reader

"Instead of aiming for children to become 'free readers' in our schools, we should help them to be free in their willingness to read."

**Encourage children to be confident by removing reading level restraints and preventing gaps from perpetuating and widening.**

Bands and schemes are colour-coded or number-based systems commonly used by schools, which differentiate books in terms of 'levels', 'stages' or 'ages' to give graduated progressions of reading. Many opt for them because of their convenience, alignment with phonics programmes, and the benefits they are believed to provide in developing skills such as fluency, decoding and comprehension.

Although there are advantages to them, some criticisms include that they can: often have uninspiring content and/or a uniform appearance; discourage and demotivate children by delaying their access to 'real' books and the real world when used in isolation; negatively affect children's perceptions of reading by turning it into a 'race'; and lead to children and parents comparing reading progress against other children.

Another thing to be aware of is the term 'free reader', which is used in schools to refer to children who have progressed through each level to complete the course and can now choose to read from a wider selection. But for those who haven't, this labelling reinforces feelings of being stuck on the scheme when the only way to relieve themselves from it is to read books they have not chosen.

Ensure that every child has choice in the books they read in school and at home, or is supplemented with books to read for pleasure to complement the banded books they read.

**#EveryChildAFree Reader**

# Bibliotherapy Books

"Reading can be the best medicine for children's minds and moods."

**There has never been a more important time to help children to find ways to support their mental health and wellbeing, so discover how to harness the power of books as a tool to do so with a practice called bibliotherapy.**

Reading can help children to feel happier in their lives and cope with a range of challenges. This is because it has many health benefits, such as reducing anxiety and depression, and building self-esteem. It can also transport children elsewhere and encourage them to escape into their imaginations.

Bibliotherapy involves carefully choosing the right books to introduce at the right times to children in the hope that they will be helpful. This includes the expression of emotions, the development of social skills and when handling difficult situations. It can be used with individuals, groups or classes.

Through reading, children can identify their emotions in a safe and supportive space. By discussing characters' experiences, they can learn to recognise their own feelings and explore ways of managing them. Books can also be used to teach children about social skills and appropriate ways to interact with others. Discussing the ways in which characters navigate a range of social situations can help children to develop empathy and understand different perspectives.

Seeing characters who overcome challenges can help children to feel less alone, provide them with a sense of hope and comfort, and encourage them to persevere through their own struggles.

It's essential that you pre-read the books you intend to use to consider their content, and if anything might need parental input or consent.

**Teaching tip**

Invest in your own collection of bibliotherapeutic books for your classroom or school. Think about how these can be included in your PSHE curriculum.

**#Bibliotherapy Books**

15

# Empathy-Boosting Books

"Empathy is an essential ingredient of every classroom."

**Empathy is described as the glue that holds society together. But in a world that can seem more concerned with selfies and selfishness, it can sometimes feel like its existence is in doubt. Find out how to embed empathy through reading in this impactful idea...**

Reading does far more than boost educational outcomes: it can also encourage empathy. Through 'book-bonding', books invite children to put themselves in others' shoes to understand characters' thoughts, experiences and emotions.

Reading a range of diverse books that showcase different cultures, experiences and perspectives can also help children develop an inclusive and open-minded approach to the world around them. This can foster a sense of respect for others, and encourage them to be empathetic to those who are different from themselves.

By supporting children to love reading, we can help them become compassionate and ethical citizens. Offer reading experiences that:

- have high-quality writing, illustrations and characters whom readers care about;
- help children to understand characters' motivations and their feelings;
- help develop key skills, e.g. perspective taking, emotion recognition and active listening;
- widen their real-world knowledge and tackle topics for which public empathy may be lacking, like refugees and homelessness;
- dig deep and provide insight into other challenging life circumstances, such as grief, bereavement, mental illness and disabilities;
- explore themes about building understanding between individuals and communities;
- confront current perceptions by offering alternative perspectives.

**#EmpathyBoosting Books**

# Re-Read

"Children have said that the second, third, or even tenth(!) time round was more special."

**Reconsider the value of repeated reading so that when those words of 'Can we read it again?' are asked, you'll embrace it and enjoy the re-reading ride instead of having feelings of despair.**

Do the children in your class love reading the same books again? Or are they one-time-only readers? With so many books and so little time, it may seem a touch tedious or trivial to reach back to the bookshelf, but repetitive reading is something to support.

If children are struggling to find something new to read next, reassure them they can return to books they've previously read. This is because re-reading provides another opportunity to enjoy a book, in the same way that you might rewatch a film or a TV show, or listen to a song over and over.

Some children enjoy revisiting books because they become familiar with understanding the story and the characters. When they re-read, they already know what to expect, which helps them to not only read with added confidence but enhances the overall reading experience by making it more enjoyable. For others, re-reading can provide a sense of relaxation, comfort and security, especially in times of stress and uncertainty.

Re-reading also offers opportunities to find new levels and layers — both in the book and in themselves as readers. They may notice details they didn't before, find a deeper appreciation of the themes and connections to the characters, and recognise how they've personally changed since last reading it.

**Teaching tip**

Repeated reading may seem like something that is frequently done with children in younger year groups, but encourage teachers and readers right across the school and regardless of age or stage to re-read.

**#ReRead**

# Creating a reading classroom

**Part 2**

# Reading Classrooms

"Changing mindsets from corners to classrooms put reading at the centre of our school."

**Challenge what you've done before and change your classroom layout with this collective, rather than corner-based, concept.**

**Teaching tip**

Involve children in the choices and the conversions of turning your reading corners into reading classrooms.

Reading corners, creatively designed to be a comfortable area for children to read in, have long been a popular part of classrooms. While they provide a specific space, sometimes they can be seen as separate and the most important element is missed out from them: books.

I believe we should have reading *classrooms* rather than just reading corners. This small but significant change in phraseology leads to seismic shifts in teachers' thinking where reading becomes the central component to each classroom's culture.

Reading corners can also give children bias — intentionally or unintentionally — about the placement, preference and precedence we teachers put upon the books in our classrooms.

- Are books found at the front, middle, back, to one side or outside of your classroom?
- Do children have a say in where books are or is this the teacher's decision?
- Do the books 'belong' separately to one area and/or accessed only once each day?
- Can children choose to read where they like?
- Is it the sole area that children associate with reading, via a brief or rushed visit?
- Could books be located all around your classroom so children realise that reading doesn't just reside in the corner?

Asking questions like these will prompt you to consider reading classrooms where children are more likely to encounter books naturally and choose to read for enjoyment.

**#ReadingClassrooms**

# Class Book

"Every child in every school should be reading a class book with their teacher every day."

**Leave children looking forward to your class book with these ideas when next choosing yours...**

A class book is one that's read aloud by the teacher to the whole class at the same time, in the same place and at the same pace. Stories that are either standalone or the start of a series are typically selected, but the class book could also be factual, poetry, a picture book, or a graphic novel.

Class books are usually read every day for enjoyment, with the pure pleasure of reading prioritised above any teaching. This ensures that literature isn't always seen as a link for learning. However, teachers may wish to occasionally tie them in with the term or half term's topic.

When reading them, teachers and children become immersed together in these shared experiences and discussions which unites them into classroom reading communities. Reading class books also exposes children to a wider array of authors and books that they may not usually choose to read themselves.

Selecting the 'correct' class book is never simple, but it could be done by the teacher or agreed upon using democratic decision-making **(Idea 1)**. Consider a representative range when choosing class books in terms of their strength of storytelling; age-appropriateness and genre; length and language; content, concept and context; inclusivity and diversity; breadth and depth; and textual and thematic challenge.

> **Teaching tip**
>
> If you don't have enough individual copies of your class book to share, project its pages onto the board using a visualiser for children to follow along.

> **Taking it further**
>
> If you're particularly precious or protective about the 'book bond' you have with children when reading your class book, ask PPA or supply teachers to bring their own books to read when covering your class so you don't miss out on what happens, or on the book talk, in the meantime.

**#ClassBook**

# Working Wall

"Children love to see the elements of our class book come together in this web of work."

**It can be easy for children to forget what happens when you're reading your class book, especially if characters or settings change frequently. Help children, particularly those who struggle to remember key details as you're discussing, to track its threads and recap them using this idea.**

**Teaching tip**

Working walls should be individual to each classroom as different books will require different features. Prevent it from becoming static by ensuring it's ever-evolving and includes children's contributions.

Working walls can be revolutionary to revisit previous readings of your class book **(Idea 17)**, embed new information about it over time and model vocabulary, whilst also providing a visual reference to the reading journey that children are experiencing as it unfolds. As a class, update the working wall regularly. This could be done every day after each chapter or a couple if they are short, or after each chunk of action or double-page spread if it's a factual, picture or poetry book.

Here are some suggested features:

- physical copies of the class book to borrow;
- images of the front cover, blurb and inside elements like maps or illustrations;
- author information and any communication or dialogue you've had with them;
- new vocabulary with definitions;
- character profiles;
- plot points and key events;
- setting descriptions;
- themes and connections within the book and to other literature they have read;
- sticky note summaries of chapters;
- children's observations, predictions, responses to others' questions and reviews;
- comprehension questions posed by the teacher and children's answers to these;
- 'ask the author' questions written by the children to send to the author/illustrator.

**Bonus idea** ★

Include QR codes to scan and see recorded videos of children reading extracts of your class book to capture their expression and fluency.

**#WorkingWall**

# Classroom Collections

"They reflect the overall importance given to reading by schools."

**Situated where their name suggests, classroom collections are invaluable in providing children with a steady supply of literature all day, every day.**

In addition to regular access to the school library, each classroom should also have its own collection of reading material. This allows children to have constant contact with literature, and provides a place where they know they can take something suitable to read at any time during the school day.

Classroom collections should feature a wide and representative range of fiction, non-fiction, poetry, picture books and graphic novels, including classics, new, inclusive and diverse books. Include areas for child-authored books also to encourage them to read their own and others' written work. Consider how children can choose and chat about the reading materials, as well as being responsible for taking care of them and learning skills like these to use on a larger scale in shared spaces such as the school library.

Remember that classroom collections are not a direct replacement for the school library, more so they are a subset of it where books are changed between the two continually and they support each other.

**Teaching tip**

Refrain from organising classroom collections as teachers. When children create them, they use and look after them more. Even very young ones can take ownership with sorting and showcasing books, and returning them to agreed places when finished with them.

**Taking it further**

As a class, start the school year by completely reorganising your collections as a community-building activity, so children feel that they truly own them.

**Bonus idea**

Take trips with teachers and support staff to your local and schools' library services, bookshops and charity shops to chat about, choose and continually refresh reading material in classroom collections.

**#ClassroomCollections**

# Currently Reading

"I can see the children's reading choices all in one go; it's like a collaborative whole class reading record!"

**Stay on top of the books that children are currently reading with this idea which connects them, shares their choices and acts as a source of inspiration and a spark for book conversation.**

This is a simple but effective idea that starts with setting up a designated display in your classroom for children to track the titles of the books they are reading and who it's written or illustrated by. Online platforms could also be used for them to share their reading choices with their peers and teachers.

IS CURRENTLY READING

Having this display allows anyone in your classroom to check out what's being read by everyone at once.

In addition to this, children can also use it as a way to discover ideas for what to read next. By seeing what their peers are reading, they can receive new recommendations for books, genres and authors that they may not have otherwise considered, which helps to expand their reading horizons.

**#CurrentlyReading**

# Book Buddies

"I don't just read with my Book Buddy, I feel like I've also made a new friend."

**Bring benefits to pairs of pupils with this support system which builds positive reading relationships and a sense of responsibility, as well as developing their social skills at the same time.**

Book Buddies is when children are teamed up in twos by teachers to meet regularly (optimally weekly or fortnightly) to read and talk about reading together. This could be with your class where they stay in their usual classroom, or across year groups or key stages, with half of the children in one class swapping with half in another.

During these times, teachers could plan for their children to:

- chat about their class book or those that they're independently reading;
- review what they've read and make recommendations to each other;
- explore classroom collections and the school library;
- complete creative activities.

But before this happens, you'll need to identify the combinations of children in your class that you think would work well or discuss the duos with their teacher if you're splitting classes to mix and match.

Consider also the frequency, duration and most convenient times for these meets to take place, the need for them to be timetabled and the logistics for children to go between classes. Selecting the same day and time every week or fortnight will help everyone to know when to expect subsequent sessions.

**Teaching tip**

If you have similar-aged Book Buddies and duplicate copies of books, encourage them to team up to read it together.

**Taking it further**

Join forces with Book Buddies at another school in your community for cross-collaboration.

**Bonus idea** ★

On occasions, try **#ReadingRotations** where instead of children moving classes, teachers switch places with each other throughout the school in order to visit different year groups and read aloud to them.

**#BookBuddies**

# Reading Recommendations

"Peer and teacher recommendations are strong signs of reading for pleasure success."

**Reading recommendations are incredibly powerful in building classroom and school communities who are buzzing about books!**

**Teaching tip**

Use rotas to track the children who have made reading recommendations to the class and to decide who is next.

**Taking it further**

Share reading recommendations, reviews and ratings of books across the school using an online platform such as Padlet for classes to comment on each others' choices and collaborate as a reading community.

This usually begins with teachers making recommendations to children, but as book talk becomes more conversational in the classroom, this can shift to children making them to their teachers. The ultimate aim is for reading recommendations to be reciprocal, or peer-to-peer, with children making them to their classmates, teachers making them to their colleagues, and classes and schools making them to each other. These can be infectious in getting others reading, and when recommendations are reverberating around a school, it is a sign that the school is well on its way to creating a thriving reading culture.

Effective ways to encourage these include:

**Teacher-to-child:** The best way is by talking about the books you're reading. Personalised sticky notes are also effective for teachers to recommend books to children. To do this, the teacher selects a book that they think a certain child would enjoy, writes a brief note explaining why, attaches it to the book and leaves the book on their table for them to discover.

**Teacher-to-child/child-to-teacher: Shared Shelves** are a great way for teachers and children to share their reading recommendations with each other. Teachers and pupils can display books they wish to recommend in a visible location, such as in a classroom or school library. They can then attach comment cards to the shelf below each book, similar to those found in bookshops, and

**#Reading Recommendations**

hand-write a review. As children's confidence increases, they can also contribute their own comment cards and share their own reading recommendations with their peers.

**Child-to-teacher:** There are many ways that children can recommend books to their teachers and have a say in what they read in class. They can suggest books that they would like to read as class books. Teachers can create a list of potential choices and children could vote for them using Children's Choice **(Idea 1)**.

**Child-to-teacher:** Create **Book Boards** of images of forthcoming and recent releases **(Idea 46)** in classrooms and corridors. Ask children to add their comments to these displays about those they are most excited about reading, explaining which ones they'd like the school to purchase and why.

**Peer-to-peer:** Writing mini-reviews on sticky notes or review charts to place inside the front covers of books they have read is a way for children to comment on books. To do this, children can write their first name, year group, a starred rating and three words to describe their thoughts. This simple strategy helps others who pick up the book to see what those who have read it thought about it.

**Peer-to-peer:** Create a Pupil to Peer promotion area in your classroom. To do this, designate a specific area in your classroom where individuals or groups of children can choose their favourite books and present them to the rest of the class. This area should be eye-level and easily accessible for other children to browse and borrow from. Children can attach sticky notes to the covers of the books with reasons why they have chosen them, a short review of the books and a rating. They can also talk about their area to the rest of the class, sharing their thoughts on the books they have chosen and why they think their classmates would enjoy them. After a while, change the display over with a new collection of books chosen by different children.

> **Bonus idea** ★
>
> **Use Reading Representatives (Idea 55)**, Reading Assemblies **(Idea 56)** or children chosen by Reader Recognition **(Idea 69)** to make 'Reading Recommendations' in classrooms or across the school.

# Book of the Week

"This has been a huge hit as children can try the book out before committing to reading it."

**Show off and spread the word about a selected book every week by giving it a special pride of place in your class.**

Display a chosen book in your classroom as the 'Book of the Week'. This could be a teacher's recommended read, a new addition, a much-loved but now neglected book or the first in a series.

By highlighting a particular one each week, you can expose children to nearly forty different books, genres, authors and illustrators over the school year. Choosing a 'Book of the Week' also encourages children to engage with the text throughout the week to try a taste of it and after getting a glimpse, they will want to pick it up beyond this weekly window too.

Make sure to include a range of fiction, non-fiction, poetry, picture books and graphic novels as your 'Book of the Week'. Sample it as a class using First Chapter Friday **(Idea 27)**, and set up Sign Out Sheets **(Idea 28)** next to it as a waiting list to record reading reservations of those children who want to continue reading it.

You could link your 'Book of the Week' choice to commemorate significant individuals, historical events, cultural celebrations and national awareness days, weeks or months.

#BookOfTheWeek

# Reading Responses

"Children's own responses reveal far more about their reading and enjoyment of it."

**What's the point of reading records if they put off reading for pleasure? Flip the focus to make it fun instead of forced and help children to develop autonomy, independence and a real willingness to read.**

Every child is different and has their own unique reading preferences. So, they should be the ones responding to their reading in their own ways, but it is adults who are often asked to sign records to show how much children have read.

**Teaching tip**

Remember that there isn't always a need for children to respond every time that they've read a book.

There are many creative ways in which children can respond to reading that don't require adult approval and it's important for teachers to respect and support children to find approaches that work for them.

Alternative approaches could include:
- Contributing to class discussions or talking to friends, family or school staff about the books they've read.
- Writing in different ways (e.g. blogs, reviews, poems or songs) to express their feelings.
- Documenting their reading lives in journals, diaries or scrapbooks **(Idea 26)** without a set format to follow or intervention from teachers or parents.
- Designing drawings, paintings or other types of artwork inspired by the books they've enjoyed.
- Making videos using technology to share their thoughts and opinions with others.
- Putting on performances or plays based on books to bring the story to life.

**Taking it further**

For further ideas on responding to reading, see Reading Roundups **(Idea 25)**, Reading Route **(Idea 31)**, and Reading Reviews **(Idea 45)**.

**#ReadingResponses**

# Reading Roundups

"The children in my class come alive when they can see what others are reading."

**See the changing reading culture in your class by collecting up your children's current self-selected reading choices and capturing them all in one collection.**

Each month, ask your class to arrange the books they are currently reading so they are sitting side-by-side on a flat surface such as the floor or a table with their covers facing upwards.

When everybody has spread out their books, take a photo directly from above looking down on all their books laid out. This bird's-eye view is a great way to gather together and gain an insight into the individual choices of literature that children are choosing to read. You may also want to ask children to attach a sticky note to the cover of their book with their name on to show whose book is whose.

Use the remainder of the time to talk to them about their current book choices and observe which books, authors and genres are often chosen. At first, you may be the one leading the discussion but as children become more confident, they could take over this role.

Send your reading round-ups to other classes and schools in your community. Does it inspire them with suggestions of books that they want to read? Can they work out which one belongs to each class?

#ReadingRoundups

# Reading Scrapbook

"One of the best things we've tried to get children motivated and talking about reading."

**Reading scrapbooks can rejuvenate the ways in which talking and thinking about books happens in your classroom whilst also keeping a record of those that children have enjoyed reading.**

Creating a reading scrapbook is a fun and engaging way for children to review the books they've read as a class, reflect on their experiences, and celebrate their love of reading in your classroom.

Each week, a different child could add a new page to your scrapbook to build up a bank of recommended books for the children to look through and use the next time they are wondering which book to read.

Within the pages of your reading scrapbook, children could:

- Share their thoughts and opinions, along with pictures or other visual elements.
- Write short summaries, reviews and commentaries.
- Create artwork of the covers, characters and memorable scenes.
- Describe how events, characters or themes relate to their lives or the world around them.
- Take pictures of themselves reading or engaging with the books they have read.
- Include anything else that is linked, for example: extracts, vocabulary, questions and quotes.

Remember that there's no right way or wrong way for children to complete it.

**Teaching tip**

Start your scrapbook with some pages to show children the kinds of things that they can include!

**Taking it further**

Set up a system for updating your class's reading scrapbook. Could children complete their entry at certain points during the day or take it home if they'd like to do it there?

**Bonus idea** ★

Issue every child with a scrapbook if you have enough resources available. Send it up with them each year so they can look back on the reading routes they've been on as they progress through your school.

**#ReadingScrapbook**

# First Chapter Friday

"When we do First Chapter Friday, I want to be first on the list to borrow the book next."

**Give children a preview of a range of books in your classroom collections through this popular, scaffolded approach and I'm sure they'll be scrambling straightaway to get them afterwards!**

First Chapter Friday is a great way to build excitement for reading and give children a sense of a book's content, writing style and overall themes.

Here's how it works:

1 At the start of the week, choose a book that you'd like to introduce to children. It can be a new book or one that you've read before.
2 Create a 'before buzz' about the book with children by promoting it in different places throughout the week in their classroom and around the school.
3 On a Friday, set aside specific time to read the first chapter of the book aloud to your class. You can also choose to have one of the children read out the first chapter if they prefer.
4 After reading the first chapter, engage children in discussion by encouraging them to ask questions and make predictions about what might happen in the rest of the book.
5 Give children opportunities to check out the book from your classroom collections or borrow a copy from the school library if they are interested in reading it on their own.

'Does it have to be on a Friday?' I hear you ask. No, any day of the week works well!

#FirstChapterFriday
#FirstPageFriday

# Sign Out Sheets

"The children take special care of the books in my classroom because of sign out sheets."

**Using sign out sheets for reading reservations is an easy and effective way for teachers to encourage equal opportunities and keep track of who is borrowing which books in the classroom.**

We've all been left feeling a little frustrated after spending time trying to track down the location of missing books in our classrooms, particularly if we've bought or brought in some of them ourselves.

To never be unsure about a book's whereabouts again and to manage the flow of books in your classroom, use sign out sheets. These allow children to 'reserve' a book that someone else is currently borrowing, ensuring they have the opportunity to read it when it becomes available. It also shows the levels of supply and demand.

Create a sign out sheet that lists all of the books that are in your classroom collection. Include the titles and authors, as well as columns for the child's name and the dates to fill in when taken out and returned.

Encourage children to make reading reservations when they want to borrow books that are already on loan by simply adding their name to the sign out sheet next to the book that they want to read. Make sure to keep track of who is next in line to borrow each book and notify them when it is their turn.

Sign out sheets could be a physical sheet of paper or an online spreadsheet, depending on what works best for your classroom.

**Teaching tip**

Ask children to take on the role of 'librarians' and update the sign out sheets themselves to reflect the current availability.

**#SignOutSheets**
**#Reading**
**Reservations**

# Reading Reflections

"It's incredible to reflect on all of the reading experiences we've had throughout the year."

**Reflecting is an important part of the reading process for children. The end of the year is the prime time to look back at the time they have spent in your class and reinforce the importance of reading.**

**Teaching tip**

Information from children's reflections could also be included to create more meaningful end-of-year experiences such as yearbooks or presentations to show in leavers' assemblies.

**Taking it further**

Make sure to also reflect on children's reading development in their end-of-year school reports **(Idea 95)**.

As the school year comes to a close, it's worthwhile to recount the children's reading experiences and reminisce about all the reading-related experiences you have shared together as a class.

You might wish to write a letter of reflection to your class to help them to think about all they have achieved with reading. Letters like these are a personalised way to recognise their progress and growth, share some of the highlights from the year, and encourage children to continue reading over the summer holidays and into the next school year by suggesting some books that they might enjoy.

Children could also reply to your letter with their own reading reflection commenting on the best parts of the year such as what they've enjoyed, felt most proud of or improved upon.

Reading your class's own reflections will help you, as the teacher, to understand what they felt was most important about your year of reading together. Often, they will mention something that you may have completely forgotten about, and you should make a note of this to include it in the following year with the next cohort of children that you teach.

Reflecting on your class's reading journey will not only leave a legacy on the children as they recognise they're a reader in their own way, but also ensures that they'll always remember you as a reader teacher.

**#Reading Reflections**

# Reading Resolutions

"They love making them as they provide such a sense of achievement and aspiration for all."

**People make New Year's resolutions every year, so adapt this concept for children to create their own reading resolutions in your classroom to complete over the course of the coming year.**

The fresh start feeling of a new school year in September gives us a great opportunity to explore and experience new things in the classroom, and setting reading resolutions can really help children to revitalise and relish their reading.

Explain what a reading resolution is: a promise to yourself to do something differently about reading, and how to make one, including the kinds of things to consider. For example, some children might set their sights on reading more, while others may want to widen their horizons and read different genres, formats or authors which are currently outside their comfort zones.

Ask the children to record their reading resolutions in a concise way, such as 'This year, my reading resolution is...'. Establish that they are personal to each child, and that everyone's will be different.

Model the SMART (Specific, Measurable, Achievable, Relevant and Timely) approach to guide their goals and set clear targets to work towards. After this, encourage children to come up with suggested strategies to help them and others to reach their resolutions.

**Teaching tip**

Display children's reading resolutions in a prominent place to help them to stay motivated and see the progress they are making.

**Taking it further**

Children could also create their resolutions in a variety of formats, such as in the style of a bookmark.

**Bonus idea** ★

As well as using this at the start of the school year in September, align it with making New Year's resolutions on your return after the Christmas holidays in January as a halfway point to take stock.

# Reading Route

"They are a lovely visual reminder to look back at what we've read."

**Timelines are a superb tool to visually sequence events, so why not create one to record the moments and milestones your class have reached along their reading journey with you during the year?**

At the start of the year, assign an area in your classroom for your display. This could take the form of a wall or window display, or a washing line. Once decided, map out a route and split it into monthly sections for the school year from September to July. Make it as simple or elaborate as you like, depending on the space and materials you have, and involve children in its design and maintenance.

As your class reads your class books **(Idea 17)** and encounters new reading experiences throughout the year, add dates, descriptions, photographs and markers to the display to represent these. Use a range of cut-out images or physical objects to symbolise different books or activities. For example, you could use cover images to illustrate each book your class reads, or a picnic basket to show your visit to a literary festival **(Idea 80)**.

To make it even more interactive, you could also encourage children to add their own markers or notes to the display as they read throughout the year. This will keep the display current and give them a sense of accomplishment as they see all the reading they've done over the course of the year.

**#ReadingRoute**

# Super Readable Books

"Books like these meet so many children's needs. I really wish I'd known about them sooner!"

**Having 'super readable' books in the classroom can be a valuable resource for all readers so use books with unique accessibility features to help every child experience the joy of reading.**

There are now a range of publishers who specialise in producing super readable books to break down the barriers that can stop children from reading. They are designed with features such as dyslexia-friendly fonts, wider line spacing and high-contrast colours. By providing these books in your classroom, you create an inclusive learning environment where all feel supported and able to participate.

Other benefits to improve readability include: greater separation between text and illustrations; clear, uncluttered layouts; expert editing to ensure comprehension and accessibility; and non-patronising content matched to the age of the reader not their assumed 'reading level'.

They are also often shorter in length than traditional books. This can make them more manageable and helpful for building readers' resilience and stamina. Finishing a book, no matter the length, can be a great source of pride for readers. By completing shorter books more quickly, children will feel a greater sense of achievement and be more motivated to continue reading.

Written and illustrated by a range of award winners and bestselling names that readers will recognise, they also provide the perfect stepping stone to reading other books from the same people.

**Teaching tip**

While having a separate section for super readable books can help readers to search for them, include them alongside others on your shelves. This avoids singling out any books or segregating readers.

**Taking it further**

Recommend these books to parents and families so they are aware of them and look out for them the next time they are buying or borrowing.

**#SuperReadable Books**

# Reading Role Play

"Role play helps to bring reading to life and make it memorable."

**Drama can sometimes feel daunting, but combining reading with role play can be a fun and engaging way to bring books to life and make it more enjoyable for children in the classroom.**

**Teaching tip**

Teaching techniques that you may already be familiar with such as freeze-framing, hot-seating, Role on the Wall and conscience alleys can all be adapted to reading contexts.

**Taking it further**

Set up role play areas based on books that your class has read to immerse them in the plot and settings.

**Bonus idea** ★

Try to get involved as the enjoyment can be significantly enhanced when teachers take part too!

In the Early Years, children often take part in play, using their imaginations to explore the world around them. As children grow older, however, it tends to become more structured and they may become more inhibited in their participation. This may be due to a variety of factors, such as increased pressure to perform or conform to certain expectations.

It's important to encourage and support children's play and creativity at all stages of development, and reading for pleasure can offer lots of authentic and creative contexts for children to engage in role play.

Pretend play with costumes, props and puppets can help children express and understand their emotions. It can also help them to develop empathy by considering the perspectives of others.

Give children opportunities to create their own interpretations of stories and to act out their favourite scenes or characters with their classmates. This builds confidence, critical thinking and collaboration.

Reading aloud and storytelling can also be powerful ways for children to engage in role play. Encourage them to take turns reading parts of their books out loud to practise their fluency and expression.

#ReadingRolePlay

# Book Match

"We've bookmarked Book Match on our computers so children can easily search for similar books."

**We all get stuck in a reading rut from time to time so help children out when they feel like this with this idea that can help them to reach out and read other authors, books and series that are much like the ones they already know and love.**

We all know that feeling when children love a certain author, series or book, but what can they and you do when it seems they've read everything that an author has ever written, completed the series, or re-read the book for the umpteenth time?

One of the challenges for teachers is having the time to read books in order to recommend them the next time someone asks 'What should I read next?'. But I may just have the solution to that particular problem.

Check out my #BookMatch for similar suggestions and books for fans of popular authors, series and books at: www.thereaderteacher.com/bookmatch. These are recommendations from a representative range of creators that have similar styles to the ones children like. Using the free printable posters, introduce children to a wide variety of options beyond what they already read, which widens their reading repertoires, helps them to self-select and encourages them to experiment with trying something new.

### Teaching tip

No two readers are the same and different criteria for each child should be considered when bookmatching.

### Taking it further

Create your own Book Match posters based on books, authors, or series that children enjoy in your classroom. Display them around your school to help others to find their next favourite books.

### Bonus idea ★

If there are any books that children would like to read that you don't have in your school, ask them to request it using a 'Reading Request' sheet **(Idea 11)**.

**#BookMatch**

# Topic Texts

"We always need to be aware of the breadth of books we share, and how we can do so."

**Broaden children's knowledge bases by accompanying your working walls and displays for topics with 'linked literature'.**

**Taking it further**

Could children bring in a book from home or the library about your topic to add to your display?

One of the most rewarding experiences of being a teacher is seeing children's natural curiosity piqued by a topic. Increase their interest and immerse them fully into topics by making associated books about them available.

Books can provide a wealth of background knowledge, context and ideas about the topic being taught that may not be covered in the classroom. This can help children to see it in a new light through nurturing a love of learning and encouraging them to continue exploring and expanding their knowledge on their own.

For example, if they are learning about ancient civilisations, having a selection of books on different civilisations, their customs and their contributions to the world allows children to gain a more well-rounded understanding as they can compare and contrast them.

Some may also prefer to read factual texts about the topic with detailed explanations, while others may prefer fictional books that bring the subject matter to life through storytelling. By providing a range of options, teachers can help ensure that all readers have access to the resources they need to set them up for success in the classroom and beyond.

In addition to this, having a diverse selection of books can provide different perspectives. This can be especially important when teaching controversial or complex subjects, as it allows children to see multiple sides of an issue and form their own opinions.

**#TopicTexts**

# Being a reader teacher

**Part 3**

# Reading Aloud

"Reading aloud is my most favourite thing to do in my day, and in my teaching career!"

**Reading aloud is probably the most important part of what teachers can do in schools, as well as the most fun, so don't let it become a rarity with these tips and takeaways.**

It's never too early to start reading aloud to children and it's also the first step in building a reading culture. This is because when teachers read aloud, it lifts the words from the page into children's imaginations and brings books to life, transforming them from two dimensions into three.

When teachers take the time to read books aloud, it sends the strongest message that reading is valued and important in their classrooms as they create close connections and a sense of community.

Reading aloud should happen every day, optimally for a period of twenty minutes in a single sitting. This commitment allows sufficient time to read a picture book or a chapter of your class book, and time to talk about what is read to further children's comprehension and interest on a deeper and personal level.

Make sure to do the voices and act out emotions when reading aloud, and share a mixture of reading material including fiction, non-fiction, poetry, picture books and graphic novels!

# Reading By Example

"Reading by example is a revelation! When they read, you read. When you read, they read."

**Give the children in your classroom another chance to see people picking up a book through this imitative idea that will leave a lasting impression on them.**

Think about when children see you reading in the classroom. How often does it happen? What do you do when they are independently reading? Do you read by example?

Reading by example is when teachers read alongside children in the classroom. You could read a children's book or an appropriate adult's book if you prefer. The effects of doing this are infectious: when children see their teacher reading for pleasure, they want to do the same. They will also become passionately curious about what you're reading and ask you about it.

It can also help you keep up-to-date with new trends and developments in literature. By reading a variety of books, you gain a deeper understanding of different genres, writing styles and perspectives. This can be shared with children to help expand their literary horizons.

Finally, reading by example can also serve as a form of self-care or professional development for teachers. It can provide a much-needed break from the demands of the classroom, allowing you to recharge and refocus. It can also be a source of personal enjoyment and fulfilment, helping you to maintain a positive and healthy work-life balance.

By making time to read your own books at the same time that children read theirs, you can benefit personally and professionally, while also promoting a culture of reading in the classroom.

> **Bonus idea** ★
>
> Try to ensure that the books you read by example are available for children to choose from in your classroom collection, as they'll want to read them after seeing them in your hands!

**#ReadingByExample**

# Reading Role Models

"Teachers who are reading role models, and love to read, teach children to love reading."

**Have you ever noticed how children seem to emulate who and what they see? Thinking carefully about how we act as reading role models can make them more likely to want to read.**

**Taking it further**

Put posters and photographs of people who are reading role models to the children around your classroom or school. These could show staff, children, families or famous figures.

Firstly, find out who children's reading role models are. Who are the people that they see reading in school and at home? What, where, when and why are they reading? How often do they see them reading? What effects does this have on them: positive or negative? Do children realise that they too are reading role models to their peers across the school?

Next, reflect on how you are a reading role model for the children in your classroom. Do the children see you reading? Do the children see you only as a teacher, a reader, or both? What do they know about your reading tastes, preferences and habits? Give children a glimpse into your literary life inside and outside school so they can learn more about you, to get to know more about themselves as readers.

Reading aloud to children on a regular basis, reading your own books alongside children in the classroom, sharing your reading experiences and encouraging them to talk about theirs, and making reading an integral part of the classroom routine, can all help children to see you as a reading role model.

**Bonus idea** ★

Run Reading Workshops **(Idea 96)** to help families understand how they can be reading role models.

There are many more ideas mentioned in this book to promote teachers and children as reading role models, such as Reading Surveys **(Idea 6)**, Book Buddies **(Idea 21)**, Reading by Example **(Idea 37)**, Reading Representatives **(Idea 55)**, Reading Assemblies **(Idea 56)**, and Reading Newsletters **(Idea 76)**.

**#Reading RoleModels**

# Know Your Books

"It makes a massive difference in knowing what you're reading is right for the children. If you don't, it won't be."

**It's critical that we know as much as we can about the books we praise, promote and put into children's hands. These three ways will ensure you make the most of knowing them inside and out.**

Knowing **about** books means being aware of aspects such as plot, characters, settings, themes and genres, as well as factual features such as the title, author, illustrator, recommended reading age, book length, and the perspective and the tense it is told in. This is the first step in gaining a good overview of the book (understanding the *who*, *what*, *where* and *when*, and its place and purpose within your curriculum).

Knowing **what** is within books means that we must delve deeper into the books to identify elements such as intertextual and cross-curricular links; authorial intent; connections to other books; sensitive and inappropriate content; and any other considerations we need to be aware of. This assists you to help children to make more informed decisions about what they read through being able to tailor your recommendations and provide the reasons when they ask *why* they should read it.

Knowing **beyond** books brings your background knowledge and understanding of how the world works together with the text to relate the content of the book to the children. Whether that be in the ways you read it, talk about it, or work with it within the curriculum, this helps you understand *how* to use the book to help children to get the most out of it.

### Teaching tip

Knowing your books is key when Reading Aloud **(Idea 36)**, so you know the perfect places to stop, and leave children wanting more.

#KnowYourBooks
#ReadingRepertoire

# Staffroom Selection

"We saw our staffroom selection was empty over the holidays as everyone was reading!"

**Spread the love of reading, reviewing, recommending, researching and reflecting on books to staff by having your very own lending library in your staffroom to get them raving about reading.**

The importance of your school's staffroom shouldn't be underestimated. As a shared space for staff to go during the school day, it's used mainly at break and lunch times for finding out the daily goings-on. But have you realised that it's also the perfect place to discuss, display and do some reading?

Reading can be a relaxing and rejuvenating activity, especially during busy workdays. Providing staff with access to books in the staffroom can give them an opportunity to take a break and recharge during their lunch breaks or other free moments.

Having a selection of children's books in the staffroom can be especially beneficial for teachers as it can give them ideas for new books to use in the classroom or for recommendations to give children and parents.

It can also be a way for staff to continue learning and growing both personally and professionally. By having a variety of books available, staff can choose books that align with their own interests and goals, whether it be for personal development or to stay up-to-date on current best practices in education.

Bringing your reading culture into the staffroom is a big step towards showing you're a reading school.

**#StaffroomSelection**

# Signature Sharing

"It generated so much more book talk than I initially expected!"

**Sharing your 'currently reading' book in your email signature is a superb conversation starter.**

Modelling the value of reading to children is essential. How often do you share your reading life with your school? How often do you show yourself as a reader? Your email signature is a great place to publicly share the books you are reading or have recently read. You could include a list of titles and authors, along with a brief description of each book.

Add a personalised signature in your settings to appear at the end of your emails, e.g. *'(Teacher name) is currently reading (Book title) by (Author/Illustrator name)'*. Each time you read a new book, update your signature to show the change of book title and author/illustrator name. Include the last book you've read and the name of your next book too: 'Last: ... by .../ Now: ... by .../Next: ... by ...'.

To make your email signature more visually appealing, you could also include a cover image of the book or a link to your review in a space such as a blog or on the book's page on a bookseller's website.

To keep your email signature current and relevant, be sure to update it regularly as you start reading new books. This will help ensure that your recommendations are always fresh.

### Teaching tip

Sometimes, you might find it difficult to keep on top of changing your email signature. Use 'This month I'm reading...' to list your reading over a longer period.

### Taking it further

List what you are currently listening to (audiobook), currently learning from (professional reading/ research), currently reading to children at home, or any reading challenges you're taking part in.

### Bonus idea

If your children have their own school-supplied email accounts, they could also create their own book sharing signatures to communicate their reading choices.

**#SignatureSharing**

# Staff Book Club

"Some staff said that our staff book was the first book they had finished in years."

**Starting a staff book club provides a supportive space to grow a reading community, collectively increase your colleagues' book knowledge and chat about children's literature, over a cuppa and a piece of cake.**

A staff book club can also be a social way to bring staff members together, allow them to get to know each other better, unwind after a busy workday and build stronger relationships with colleagues.

Here are some steps that you can follow to set up your own book club in a primary school:

1 **Identify interested participants:** First, it's important to gauge interest among staff members to see who might be interested in joining the book club. You could send out a survey or just ask around informally to see who might be interested.
2 **Determine the focus and format of the book club:** Will the club focus on children's literature, adult literature, or both? Will it meet in person or online?
3 **Choose a facilitator:** It can be helpful to have one person take the lead in organising and facilitating the book club. This person could also be responsible for initially selecting books, scheduling meetings and leading discussions.
4 **Select the books:** Choose a children's and/or adult's book that aligns with the focus of the book club. Consider asking for input from other members on book choices. Schools could purchase copies of the chosen book for the club, seeing it as a small price to pay for staff development, and afterwards

**#StaffBookClub**

they can be used by teachers as class books or for children to use as group sets.

5 **Set the schedule:** Determine how often the book club will meet and at what time. It can be helpful to choose a consistent day and time to make it easier for members to commit.

6 **Promote the book club:** Send out invitations to all staff members who may be interested in joining the book club. Use a sign-up sheet or online form to make it easy for people to join.

7 **Hold the meetings:** At each meeting, share your thoughts and insights about the chosen book. It can be helpful to have some discussion questions prepared in advance to guide the conversation.

> **Bonus idea** ★
>
> Share your staff book choice and your progress with parents and pupils using your communication channels. This will also increase demand from children to want to read the book so make sure to have multiple copies across the school!

# Reading and Research (R&R)

"Reading and research is a valuable and valid use of any teacher's time."

**Teachers' time is precious so take risks with this radical idea to build time into school schedules to release staff to read and research, and progress personally and professionally too.**

The benefits of reading for pleasure are well-known for children, but what about for teachers too? Not only has it been proven to reduce stress, it can also change teachers' practice and productivity. So why do we not give them the same opportunities to read and research in school that we do for children?

Teachers and schools are both incredibly busy. It's difficult to fit in all that needs to be done in a day. But providing staff with protected non-contact time to read children's books in order to use them in the classroom and research reading for pleasure pedagogy is a significant step in working towards changing your culture into that of a reading school. Consider it as continuing professional development (CPD).

Reading children's literature and researching teaching strategies around reading for pleasure can help teachers enhance their lesson planning and design more engaging and effective lessons for children. By exploring different themes, characters and plotlines, teachers can gain new ideas and perspectives that they can use to create more meaningful and relevant learning experiences for their classes.

Giving teachers dedicated time to read children's literature and research teaching strategies can also help them stay on top of the best practices in education and identify new trends and approaches that they can use in the classroom. By using literature to spark

**#ReadingAnd Research**

discussions, facilitate activities and make connections to real-world issues, teachers can better capture the attention and curiosity of children.

Providing teachers with dedicated time to read children's literature and research teaching strategies can also be a valuable investment in their professional development. It can help teachers stay motivated and engaged in their work and give them opportunities to continue learning and growing as educators.

This may not be your decision to make, so approach your Reading Lead or senior leadership team and suggest how your school can set dedicated time for staff to regularly read and research, in addition to their PPA time. Can it be built into staff meetings or somewhere else in their directed time? What about within ECT time for new teachers, or leadership and management time for subject and senior leaders?

It's tough for teachers to just become readers or researchers, so this requires some scaffolding. To start, allocate staff with reading and research tasks. This could be reading a chapter of a children's book of their choice; an extract of one that has been chosen for them; or an article of reading-related research that aligns with your school's aims. After they do this, set staff a series of questions to answer to help them to think deeper about what they have read. These reflections can be recorded on paper or online R&R diaries, which can be shared with your Reading Lead **(Idea 48)**, Head Reader **(Idea 49)**, Senior Readership Team **(Idea 50)**, and during staff-sharing sessions such as Reading Roundtables **(Idea 44)**.

**Bonus idea** ★

Supply a range of articles and chapters in your Staffroom Selection **(Idea 40)** to encourage staff to engage with reading-related research outside of this dedicated time.

# Reading Roundtables

"They give staff the chance to collaborate in order to think creatively and critically about all things reading."

**Schools can support all staff members in developing their personal and professional understanding of reading for pleasure through these shared sessions so that everyone is on the same page.**

Providing regular opportunities for staff to discuss reading can be difficult in the school day, so think about how to replace traditional meetings termly or half-termly where they can:

1 **Explore books:** By reading, recommending, talking about and sharing new and diverse books together, staff can gain insights and perspectives that they can bring back to their classrooms.

2 **Expand school and subject knowledge:** By expanding their knowledge by listening and learning to others, staff can deepen their understanding of reading for pleasure across the school.

3 **Engage in current best practice:** By sharing and discussing research-based books and articles, staff can stay up-to-date on the latest trends and techniques in developing reading for pleasure.

4 **Enhance lesson planning:** By providing a range of ideas and inspiration, staff can help each other to plan more engaging and effective reading for pleasure lessons.

5 **Event plan:** By being together all at once, staff can collaborate to organise whole school, key stage or year group reading events such as author visits and a Festival of Reading **(Idea 83)**.

You could also invite your local bookshop or library to showcase books.

**#ReadingRoundtables**

# Reading Reviews

"They help our children and teachers to form and foster healthy reading relationships together."

**Regular reading reviews benefit teachers by helping them to learn more metacognitively about children's thinking towards their reading.**

A significant part of creating and continuing a reading for pleasure culture is understanding children's reading patterns, preferences, practices and profiles, both in school and at home.

One way of doing this is through Reading Reviews that could occur either termly or half-termly. These are times of dedicated dialogue in one-to-one or small group sessions between teachers and each child in their class about their attitudes towards reading and to find out how they can be further supported on their reading for pleasure journeys. A typical reading review will take about ten minutes per person and can take place during teaching time or outside of the classroom.

Teachers and children both come to the review prepared and ready to talk together about the child's reading. Teachers can also: listen to children read; hear their thoughts and feelings about reading; and provide feedback. Often, this is when common reading-related strengths and struggles are revealed by children's comments about their difficulties and demotivations. Strategies can be suggested to successfully overcome barriers and short-term targets could also be set to track reading for pleasure progress over subsequent sessions and throughout the school year.

**Teaching tip**

Reading Reviews provide an alternative to Reading Surveys **(Idea 6)**, and could be used in conjunction with them to capture more of a complete picture of children's reading for pleasure.

**Taking it further**

Your Reading Lead **(Idea 48)** could complete the conferencing of Reading Reviews in their reading leadership time with certain children from each year group to see a sample spread across the school.

**Bonus idea** ★

Invite parents to participate in Reading Reviews with their children to talk about reading together from both a pupil and parent perspective.

**#ReadingReviews**

# Recent Releases

"It's so important to stay up to date with the current climate of children's books in the classroom."

**Around ten thousand new children's books are published in the UK every year so it's difficult to know which are worth reading or even where to start. But you can keep on top of them with these handy tips...**

The majority of new releases come out every Thursday, with the start and end of each month usually being the busiest. Set reminders and your calendar can take care of it from there. If your school is big on buying or borrowing books, get ahead by pre-ordering or reserving them at your local library or schools' service. This can result in books arriving before publication day which is a real reading surprise!

There are many websites and blogs dedicated to reviewing and recommending children's books. By visiting these, you can stay informed and get a sense of which books are worth adding to your classroom collections and school libraries.

Many publishers, authors and illustrators use social media to share information about their work. Follow them to receive notifications about their new releases.

Other ways include:

- watching people previewing and reviewing children's books on YouTube (see my channel www.youtube.com/c/TheReaderTeacher);
- listening to podcasts;
- joining online communities to chat about children's books
- receiving children's books subscriptions;
- seeing which books have won or been shortlisted for children's book awards.

**#RecentReleases**

# Reading Conferences

"I've already started to implement so many of the ideas I heard about."

**Attend or host conferences to gather reader teachers together and explore approaches to develop reading for pleasure.**

Reading conferences are large-scale events that welcome keynote speakers and delegates who can choose to attend a range of presentations, panels and workshops. They're a great opportunity to further your pedagogical knowledge and understanding of reading for pleasure because you can make contact with colleagues and see what's happening in schools on local, national and international levels.

There are increasing numbers of one-day reading conferences during the working week (or on weekends, if you wish to go in your own time), but they can also be multi-day or after-school meets.

There, you'll be inspired to network with other educators, learn from each others' experiences and exchange ideas that you can use to take back and improve reading for pleasure in your classroom. Many conferences feature exhibitors and book fairs where teachers can browse and purchase new books and reading resources, and also meet authors and illustrators.

Have you ever considered hosting or running your own reading conference at your school? Hosting a reading conference is when your school is selected as the setting for a conference managed by an external provider, such as a reading organisation or media corporation. Running a reading conference means you organise it internally from scratch. They involve different skill sets but both can benefit your school in creating and continuing its reading culture.

**Teaching tip**

Make sure to have a pen and paper handy to jot down ideas to use back in your classroom.

**#Reading Conferences**

# Leaders are readers

Part 4

# Reading Lead

"I feel so fortunate to be the Reading Lead at a school where I can help to support each child to learn how to read and to read for pleasure successfully."

**Subject leaders are crucial to a school's success in starting, securing and sustaining improvement, and recruiting a specific Reading Lead shows that you prioritise reading.**

### Teaching tip

Remember that creating and continuing a reading culture shouldn't be the sole responsibility of the Reading Lead, and having a Senior Readership Team in place can help to share the requirements evenly.

### Taking it further

With the work that it requires, depending on the size and structure of your school, you could share the role or separate it into two, having an Early Reading Lead for Early Years and Key Stage 1 (with particular expertise in or experience of phonics) and another Reading Lead for Key Stage 2.

As a Reading Lead in a primary school, you will ensure that all children have access to high-quality reading materials and that they are receiving the support they need to become proficient readers. You will work closely with teachers, leaders and support staff to initiate and implement a reading culture.

As part of your role you could:

- apply a clear and inclusive core vision for reading across the school, based on relevant research and best practice including Early Reading and phonics.
- champion and encourage children, staff, and the school community to enjoy reading, and promote this through a range of school-wide initiatives.
- oversee the reading curriculum across the school, including what should be taught and secured in each year group, as well as meet the expectations in Early Years and manage transitions.
- have a deep, diverse and up-to-date knowledge and application of children's literature to ensure that everyone has access to high-quality and engaging texts.
- audit reading resources and organise provision, and purchase when required.
- realise what progress in reading is and how to achieve and assess it.

**#ReadingLead**

- recognise the relationship between reading and the other elements of English, and how to plan successfully for these in subjects across the curriculum.
- monitor and evaluate effectively, by consistently building on practice and driving change to raise the reading engagement and attainment of everyone.
- lead by example and support reading across the school with running staff meetings, CPD, INSET, and working in partnership with parents and other people and organisations.

In addition to these, you may also be responsible for tracking and analysing data on children's reading progress and using this information to inform your work. This may include administering reading assessments, analysing test results, and using this data to identify areas of strengths and shortcomings.

**Bonus idea** ★

If a teacher is going to be newly appointed to the role of Reading Lead, try to accommodate a period of time to shadow the current person in post to ensure continuity and consistency.

# Head Reader

"Every headteacher should set out with the aim to show they are a head reader in their schools."

**Reading is everyone's responsibility. Having a Head Reader, a headteacher who's passionate about reading for pleasure, can have such a profound impact on schools in setting the tone from the top.**

**Taking it further**

Can they partner with local libraries, bookshops or other community organisations to promote reading in your school?

Having a 'Head Reader' who actively promotes reading for pleasure can help to create a culture of reading and learning in your school, and inspire pupils and staff to develop a lifelong love of reading.

Their enthusiasm and commitment can be contagious, and can have a ripple effect on reading throughout the school community, inspiring children and staff to prioritise reading in their own lives.

Is yours recognised as your 'Head Reader'? Discuss with your headteacher the ways that they can help to promote reading for pleasure in your school through their personal practice and professional policies.

Personally

- Are they seen reading for pleasure regularly and sharing their love of reading across the school in classrooms, Reading Assemblies **(Idea 56)**, or other opportunities outside of their office?
- Do they allocate amounts of time each week for your children to simply read for pleasure?
- Have they created a culture that values reading for pleasure and made it a priority by ensuring that your school library and classroom collections have a range of reading materials available?

**#HeadReader**

- Can they review and recommend books in different ways, e.g. in Reading Newsletters **(Idea 76)**?
- Do they model good reading habits and encourage children to read at home?

Professionally

- Are they a member of your Senior Readership Team **(Idea 50)** to make whole school decisions about implementing and improving reading for pleasure?
- Is reading for pleasure prioritised on your school improvement plan **(Idea 52)**?
- Do they set aside a specific Book Budget **(Idea 53)** to buy books for your school?
- What steps do they take to ensure that reading for pleasure is at the heart of learning such as introducing a Book Based Curriculum **(Idea 59)**?
- How do they provide staff with continuing professional development about reading for pleasure?

> **Bonus idea** ★
>
> Talk to your headteacher about how they can also be involved with reader recognition in your school.

# Senior Readership Team

"Working together in this way ensures that everyone is on the same page in our school."

**Nearly all schools have a senior leadership team. Just as your school has one to set the school's direction, have you considered how it could also have its own 'senior readership team' to meet regularly and make key decisions about reading for pleasure?**

The senior readership team could comprise:

- headteacher **(Idea 49)**
- deputy / assistant headteacher(s)
- reading lead **(Idea 48)**
- school librarian **(Idea 86)**
- curriculum reading champions **(Idea 51)**
- special educational needs co-ordinator (SENCo)
- key stage leaders
- year group leaders (in larger schools)

For sustained and shared success, a cohesive whole-school approach to promoting reading for pleasure is important. Therefore, the senior readership team can work together to develop a reading for pleasure policy that outlines the importance of reading for pleasure and how it will be promoted across the school. They can also support teachers in promoting reading for pleasure in their classrooms, and take the lead in planning reading events and initiatives such as book clubs and author visits.

They should also try to prioritise funding and budgeting for books **(Idea 53)**, provide staff with professional development opportunities related to reading, and work with the wider community to raise awareness about the importance of reading for pleasure and the benefits it brings to the school.

**#SeniorReadership Team**

# Curriculum Reading Champions

"Being a CRC makes me much more aware of the power and potential of reading within subjects."

**Add another layer of leadership to reading to help leaders to support their subjects and strengthen your status as a reading school.**

Within your staffing structure, you'll probably have leaders or curriculum coordinators who oversee improvement and provide guidance about specific subjects. But do they also recognise the responsibility they have for reading within their area(s)?

Ensure that subject leaders' role specifications state how each of them are also reading champions for their subject, and will work with the Senior Readership Team **(Idea 50)** to get the most out of reading.

Think about how you can help subject leaders become Curriculum Reading Champions by:

- developing their knowledge of children's literature that is appropriate to their subjects to share with teachers;
- improving their use of fiction and non-fiction text types to offer more reading opportunities;
- helping them implement reading strategies such as content area and disciplinary reading;
- helping them understand what reading in their subjects looks like for all readers.

**Teaching tip**

Provide Curriculum Reading Champions with dedicated time to read children's books themselves and discuss how to utilise them effectively with staff, as well as any training required.

**Taking it further**

Consider how your Curriculum Reading Champions can regularly reflect and report findings on reading within their subjects to staff such as in Reading Roundtables **(Idea 44)**.

**#Curriculum ReadingChampions**

# Put Reading on the Plan!

"Putting reading for pleasure on our school improvement plan sets a precedent for all."

**Empower your school to put reading in a prominent place with this idea that shows you are developing a coherent whole school strategy for promoting reading for pleasure.**

**#PutReading OnThePlan**

Highlight any reading-related targets on your school improvement plan. Are these associated with the subject of English? Do they correspond to improving reading skills such as comprehension? Are they only about the reading engagement of either boys or girls, or data-driven targets about achievements of certain 'groups'? Typically, these are the kinds of targets that you'll spot. But ask yourself: is there an emphasis on creating a whole school reading culture? Developing teachers' knowledge of texts? Budgeting for buying books? Arranging author visits, etc.?

Initiate a collaborative discussion with your colleagues, including senior leadership, about including reading for pleasure as part of your school improvement plan. Formulate an action plan, generating a series of attainable approaches, including how reading for pleasure will feature within future agendas, targets and staff's personal development plans. Think carefully how you can put what you have planned into practice, and how to embed it so that it becomes a normalised and natural part of school life.

*Placing* reading for pleasure on your school improvement plan is the first step in showing that your school invests in its importance. *Prioritising* reading for pleasure at the core of your school's improvement plan will ensure that it stays deeply rooted and developed within your school's culture.

# Book Budget

"Buying books is an essential investment for success in a school."

**Reading cultures cannot exist without a certain level of commitment and consistency to buying books, but this comes at a cost. A book budget shows that you place priority on them.**

Many schools do not have ring-fenced finance for buying books, leaving teachers little choice but to spend their own money. Has your school got protected premiums for some subjects but none for books? Funds for purchasing books need greater preservation by a higher power than school management, but there are things we can do to try to budget for books.

**Taking it further**

Hand a certain level of control to the children for them to decide. Giving them greater 'reading responsibility' will mean that books are bought and chosen more carefully.

Establish your school's 'Book Budget' by:

1 **Determining your needs:** Before setting a budget, it's important to assess your school's wants, how many books you need, and to consider the state of the overall budget.
2 **Researching prices:** Compare the prices of different types of books from different retailers. This will help you to determine the average cost and set a realistic budget.
3 **Allocating funds:** Once you've done this, allocate a specific amount to the book budget. This should be sufficient to cover the cost of the books you need, but it's important to be mindful of other priorities and that you're not overspending.
4 **Setting priorities:** This is how the budget will be used. This might include purchasing books for classroom collections or the school library, or investing in books for teachers.
5 **Reviewing and adjusting:** You may need to adjust the budget if prices change, or you may need to review and reallocate more funds if the budget is insufficient to cover your needs.

**#BookBudget**

# Reading Audit

"They help us to step back, take stock and look at the bigger picture."

**Review the reading for pleasure practice in your school to assess where your positives, problems and possible pitfalls are and to make informed decisions about where to allocate resources.**

A reading audit is a systematic evaluation of the school's reading for pleasure culture, including its curriculum, resources and assessment. Carrying one out can help your school to identify its strengths and shortcomings in reading for pleasure and make necessary improvements. This could be led by your Reading Lead **(Idea 48)**, Head Reader **(Idea 49)** or Senior Readership Team **(Idea 50)**.

Find out from children and staff across the school about their reading for pleasure experiences inside and outside the classroom, from what to where they read. Other sources of information that can be drawn on for their value in an audit include Reading Surveys **(Idea 6)** and Reading Reviews **(Idea 45)**.

Once you've completed your audit, analyse the results. Celebrate what's going well and give everyone recognition for their successes, no matter how small they think they are.

Next, assess any areas you would like to improve. Develop an action plan by prioritising the issues based on their importance and impact and working with relevant stakeholders to pinpoint potential solutions. Implement the plan in a timely manner to address the identified issues and prevent any further problems from arising. It may be necessary to monitor progress and make adjustments as needed.

After the plan has been put into action, it's important to review the results and follow up in the future.

**#ReadingAudit**

# Setting up a reading school

**Part 5**

# Reading Representatives

"Our reading representatives are an absolute asset to our school community."

**Mould leaders of the future by giving children a chance to take on this responsibility to have their voice heard.**

#Reading
Representatives
#ReadingReps

Reading Representatives are a learner leadership team who are chosen to represent their peers, act as ambassadors and meet regularly to discuss ways in which they can promote the love of reading for pleasure in the school. They can apply, volunteer or be voted into the role.

Reading Reps could be responsible for:

- reading regularly with and to others
- recommending books and authors to others in classroom collections and the school library
- reviewing books as a panel before they enter classroom collections and the school library
- selecting books to replenish school stock
- spending the Book Budget **(Idea 53)** to understand the buying process
- looking after classroom collections or the school library as librarians
- designing reading displays to develop a visual reading culture across the school
- contributing to the recognition of reading in your School Development Plan
- planning, organising and helping out at whole school reading events and author visits
- delivering Reading Assemblies **(Idea 56)**
- celebrating other children's reading successes
- helping fundraise for books and reading resources
- visiting local libraries and reading organisations to build reading relationships with others
- attending and presenting at reading events both inside and outside of school
- communicating about reading to the school, e.g. Reading Newsletters **(Idea 76)**.

# Reading Assemblies

"Reading assemblies help everyone look at, listen to and love books in our school."

**Assemblies are an important part of school life. Make sure they aren't a missed opportunity with this idea that brings reading for pleasure to a whole school audience.**

An approach that can be applied universally across your school is reading assemblies, when staff dedicate assemblies as a time to read to a hall full of children, who hang onto every word and become lost in the act of reading together. This can be through the pages of a picture book, a poem, a short story, or even an extract from a fiction or non-fiction text; some genres will work better than others.

Different reading assemblies for different key stages may need to be considered in your school so content can be adapted accordingly. You may wish to use reading assemblies to introduce children to a new book each time, or to revisit old favourites.

Encourage a variety of staff to participate including teachers, support staff and the senior leadership team. Ask learner leadership teams (School/Eco Council, Digital Leaders, Reading Representatives **(Idea 55)** etc.), to also lead reading assemblies about an issue they are raising awareness about. Classroom sessions could also take place after reading assemblies to build on what's been read, linking learning and developing deeper discussion.

### Teaching tip

Projecting the text and illustrations onto a screen will help children to feel more included, especially if you invite them to join in as you read aloud.

### Taking it further

Plan out a reading assemblies calendar, choosing books to commemorate significant individuals, historical events, festivals and cultural celebrations, and national awareness periods over the year, such as World Book Day, Remembrance Day, Black History Month, Anti-Bullying Week, LGBT+ History Month and International Women's Day.

### Bonus idea ★

Post what you're reading in reading assemblies on your School Socials **(Idea 77)** and communication channels to build a 'book bridge' between school and home.

**#ReadingAssemblies**

# Reading Spine

"Our school's reading spine supports us to feel safe in our knowledge of sharing the best books we can."

**Creating your own school reading spine helps children to love, live and learn through literature and gives them a reading guarantee before secondary school.**

Schools with reading spines build a collective, common core of books that all children will experience and enjoy throughout their time there.

Firstly, think about the books you want to fill your classrooms, corridors, collections and curriculum. Some might be used to teach, some might be used as whole class reads and some for independent reading. Sometimes they may link to the subjects and topics studied, but not always.

Start small with a short, minimum collection of core texts selected for each year group to carefully curate your own school-specialised reading spine. Use staff development sessions to consult with each other about which books teachers wish to supplement as their own choices.

Ensure that your spines are fluid and flexible from year to year, meaning that teachers can add or remove texts, after discussion. This could be when different or more recently published texts align closer to your cohort of children's reading requirements. Doing this will also result in ever-evolving and better book talk between teachers as it encourages them to become more critically aware of the texts and the reasons for reading them in the classroom.

My Top *100 Recommended Reads* booklists on TheReaderTeacher.com/year-groups are a good place to start for suggestions to select age-appropriate books for each year group.

**#ReadingSpine**

# Whole School Books

"We love reading and working on our whole school book. It brings us all together in the best ways."

**This idea connects everyone around the common threads to explore the same book, at the same time, but in different ways.**

A 'whole school book' is a text that is used with every year group from Nursery to Year Six because they have a uniquely universal appeal, are accessible because children of all ages can read them on many multi-layered levels and everyone can take away something different from their pages.

**Taking it further**

Contact the author(s) and illustrator(s) of your whole-school text to show them the work that has been completed based on their book.

Whole school books could be fictional or factual, as well as wordless. Picture books are a popular choice because they offer an open-ended and alternative way of storytelling, inviting the children to make meaning from the illustrations and sense of what they see, which develops their language skills, challenges them to dive deeper into a book and to also explore exciting links with other subjects.

Whole school books work exceedingly well for entire school engagement and could be a reading strategy that is repeated annually in your school, such as to celebrate national awareness days or weeks like World Book Day.

**Bonus idea** ★

Whole school books could also provide the inspiration for whole school trips based on their content. These will not only act as shared experiences but as vehicles to bring books to life.

When thinking about what to do with a whole school text, plan out many possibilities and develop ideas together, firstly within year groups and then cross-phase to support the richest possible explorations of the book. This ensures that meaningful links across the curriculum are made and maximised, as well as anticipating any difficulties. For suggestions of suitable texts, see a list of my recommended whole school books in the Appendix (page 130).

#WholeSchool Books

# Book-Based Curriculum

"Rewriting our reading curriculum to teach through texts has been the best thing we've done."

**Concentrating your curriculum around books helps to create one that's reading-rich for all.**

Teaching through texts and using a book-based approach to underpin your school's curriculum allows children to link literature to their learning. Books should regularly be the basis for English and reading lessons in your school, but are they used across the curriculum successfully to the same effect?

When considering how best to use books to link to learning, they can broadly be broken down into the following four text types:

- **Initiatory texts** help to introduce a topic and its ideas, ignite interest, and are often used over the whole time spent studying it. As core texts, they give children a central focus and act as anchors to base learning around by creating curiosity or presenting problems for them to explore further.
- **Immersion texts** complement initiatory texts by immersing children in literature linked to the topic to take them deeper into it, and greater support their skills and knowledge development.
- **Investigation texts** are particular pages of books, rather than the whole book, used as part of projects or enquiries. They convey information clearly for the purpose of research so that children can ask and answer questions about important aspects of the topic.
- **Inspiration texts** act as a model or stimulus for children to recreate learning inspired by or imitated in the same style, layout or organisation of the original text.

#BookBased Curriculum

# Reading Representation

"Seeing someone like you in a book can be truly transformative."

**Consider who and what you're reading so children can see themselves on your shelves.**

Surrounding children with literature helps them to realise that it's an essential part of their lives, and all children deserve to be able to see themselves represented in a book.

You don't need thousands of books in your school but there should be a representative range of the people, settings, backgrounds and cultures that coexist in our communities. Books are mirrors and windows to our world and doors to others (*Mirrors, Windows and Sliding Glass Doors*, Sims Bishop, 1990), and using them to inclusify (*Inclusify*, Johnson, 2020) and enhance your school's curriculum enables children to encounter people like themselves and to learn with empathy about people, places and events outside of their own experiences.

Think carefully and consciously about how reflective the range of books in your school is, in terms of representation of: age; disability; gender and gender identity; race and heritage; religion, belief and culture; sexual orientation; and socioeconomic status. Consider also the gender and race of the author, illustrator or poet; of the main character or significant supporting characters; the complexities of these characters; the visual representation of these characters; the book's settings; and the family structures shown. This is why teachers must know their books **(Idea 39)**.

Doing this means that representation and diversity are not covered tokenistically but authentically, respectfully and sensitively as an inbuilt and integral part of your curriculum.

**Teaching tip**

Make every effort to ensure that visitors, displays and other reading-related activities feature diverse characters, authors and illustrators.

**Taking it further**

Supply copies of books in a range of different languages relevant to the children and your community on your shelves for greater access, inclusion, representation and diversity.

**Bonus idea** ★

Wherever possible, select books by people who've lived the experiences they are writing about, known as #OwnVoices, to provide and portray reliable representation, and nullify the risks of promoting negative stereotypes or discrimination.

**#Reading Representation**

# Book Mapping

"It's an eye-opening experience for everyone to see where the books we read are based."

**Help children and staff to become global reading citizens and be more informed about the range of reading it provides with this idea that looks at things from an international perspective.**

As a staff, sit down together with a world map and images or physical copies of the books from your school reading spine(s), school library stock or classroom collections. Place the copies or pictures of the books in their geographical locations on the map to show where each book is set within the world, or use small sticky notes with their titles on.

What do you recognise? Are there any noticeable patterns, similarities or differences? Do you have a representative range of reading books that children and your community can relate to? Do they also reflect the realities of those that you teach? Are there any 'map gaps'? Can children read their way around the world? How are all cultures and continents covered?

As a result of seeing the bigger picture, what could you do differently? What will now be your next steps in ensuring greater text equality, inclusivity, diversity and representation across your school for readers?

#BookMapping

# Reading All Year Round

"Reading right the way throughout the year makes our school a better place to be."

**Celebrate reading all year round and make every day a World Book Day in your school.**

Think about how and when reading is celebrated within your school. Is it done regularly as part of the everyday, or only occasionally through one-off events scattered sporadically throughout the year?

Chances are that your school already celebrates World Book Day. However, if you're seeking to not only create but also continue a reading culture, reading should be recognised through a year-round approach for a comprehensive and constant immersion. Remember that books are not just for World Book Day or World Book Week.

Plan out your school's own 'Year of Reading', using a literacy calendar contributed to by all staff, to celebrate the many literary-themed events, awards and promotions throughout the year including National Non-Fiction November, National Poetry Day and the Summer Reading Challenge **(Idea 88)**. There are also a number of national awareness days, weeks and months which deserve the same 'reading response' as World Book Day. This can be done by linking to literature within lessons and/or sharing books through a whole school focus such as reading assemblies **(Idea 56)**.

It's brilliant to celebrate books at specific times such as those listed above, but for a more rounded reading experience, think about how you could also be promoting books, reading, storytelling, and authors and illustrators all year round.

**Teaching tip**

When celebrating reading, ensure that the place, power and potential of books are prioritised alongside the costumes and commerciality of these events.

**Bonus idea** ★

Think about how you can involve your local library, bookshop or other external organisations such as reading charities to provide more focused expertise and a holistic approach.

**#ReadingAll YearRound**

# Book Club

"I love going to school when I know it's Book Club. It's the best day of the week!"

**Starting a book club can be a fun, rewarding way to boost book talk and multiply the love of reading for its members. Here are some steps for setting up a successful book club in your school...**

1 **Aim it at a specific age group:** Open access to all children from the key stage(s) you have selected who'd like to attend. It may be helpful to have a numerical limit that you're able to accommodate and if too many apply, change the children in the club over termly or half-termly.

2 **Select a suitable book to read aloud:** It could be fiction, non-fiction, poetry, a picture book, a graphic novel or a mix of genres. Also, ask children for their input on what they're interested in reading and choose one using Children's Choice **(Idea 1)**. Children usually read the same book so there's a common conversation, but they could read, review and recommend books of their own to each other too.

3 **Choose an appropriate location:** Consider a comfortable and quiet space, such as a classroom or the school library.

4 **Set up a schedule:** Decide when you will meet, how often, and how long meetings will last — making sure they're regular to maintain momentum. It might be better to start with shorter meetings, such as once a week for 30 minutes, and then adjust as needed.

5 **Have fun and enjoy the experience:** In addition to reading and discussing the book, think about incorporating other interactive activities related to the book you're reading. Provide some refreshments for readers such as juice and biscuits. This makes the book club more memorable!

**#BookClub**

# Residential Reading

"Seeing the books that my teachers bring makes me want to spend the whole residential reading!"

**Take books with you to read on your residential to provide a source of entertainment during downtime and give children a different, shared experience of reading in a recreational setting.**

Every year, many children go on residential trips with their school, which provide enjoyable experiences and enduring memories through opportunities for learning outside the classroom as well as offering one of the first experiences of being away from family and familiar surroundings.

During these, the days are often filled with things to do from outdoor pursuits to team-building, but the evening activities are usually left up to the teachers to oversee. Therefore, ensure that reading is part of your residential life, as it would be in the classroom, by sharing a story every evening around the campfire, after dinner or before bedtime.

Choose carefully the book(s) that you'll read. It could be one that you're reading in the classroom and you'd like to continue. Or it could be a series of shorter stories that can be read over the time that you're away for, or it may even be a book with a residential or outdoor theme to make the most of the opportunity.

Consider how books can also provide a soothing sense of familiarity and comfort for children who may be missing home, and help them to feel more at ease in a new environment.

### Taking it further

Encourage residential skills such as teamwork and social interaction through reading. Children could have evening chats about books, swap them over to review and recommend, and read by torchlight.

### Bonus idea

Reading opportunities are everywhere you go. Bring a book for the bus to read yourself, or one to read together on the way there and back as a 'school trip story time'. Also, ask children to take something to read to keep them company on the coach for shorter journeys, like when classes go swimming.

**#ResidentialReading**

# Books At Breakfast Club

"We're always thinking about how we can share books from breakfast club to bedtime."

**By including books as an integral part of your breakfast club, schools can help children to commence every day in a healthy way and set the stage for a successful day of learning.**

Most schools provide free breakfast clubs for children to attend in the early morning where they are provided with a filling breakfast as well as having fun with their friends before the start of the school day. But have you considered how you can build on this being an essential beginning to a child's day by also serving up a love of reading at your school's breakfast club?

Books can be incorporated into breakfast clubs by having designated reading areas where children can sit and enjoy reading a book by themselves before, during or after they eat their breakfast. Create a calm and relaxing atmosphere with little lending libraries, story sacks or book boxes situated in your school hall — or another location where your breakfast club takes place. This will encourage children to not only take books to their tables and share together, but also prompt plenty of book talk **(Idea 7)** and reading recommendations **(Idea 22)**.

**#BooksAtBreakfastClub**

# Digital Reading

"Reading digitally can help to break down several significant barriers for our children."

**Digital reading is becoming an increasingly important part of children's literary lives so use this idea to exploit and explore how it can be an integral part of your reading school.**

For many people, nothing beats reading a book as you turn its pages, but we live in an increasingly digital age where children are reading more on screen than ever before. Ebooks, audiobooks and other online formats are frequently changing what, where and how they read.

Using digital devices, online platforms and apps to access reading can be the key to unlocking a lifetime love of literature. These can increase children's engagement with and enjoyment of reading; enhance their learning and digital literacy skills; and offer opportunities for greater personalisation for children with features such as text-to-speech and adaptive text.

Set up your own digital library for your classroom or school, so children can access books anywhere by scanning QR codes to listen to stories being read aloud to them, read extracts and download digital editions of newspapers or magazines that you subscribe to.

Many author visits, literary festivals and summer reading challenges are going digital in their attempts to reach wider audiences so make sure to maximise these opportunities too.

### Teaching tip

With worries about children's screen time on the rise, aim to provide a balance between digital reading and in-print reading in your classroom. Take time to do digital detoxes.

### Taking it further

In addition to using them in the classroom, there are a range of apps that can also support parental engagement and provide links with local libraries and book borrowing.

### Bonus idea ★

When watching videos in the classroom, switch on subtitles or closed captioning so children can read whilst they watch.

**#DigitalReading**

# Book Awards

"Our book awards get everyone buzzing about books."

**Get involved with national book awards and celebrate children's favourite books by holding your own classroom or school book awards, complete with a ceremony to announce the winners.**

Throughout the year, there are many children's book awards which celebrate different qualities books have, including best stories, books with facts, funny books, scientific and historical fiction, poetry, picture book illustration, diverse voices or first-time writers.

Schools can participate in book awards in different ways. They can take on the role of being a book judge in awards like the Royal Society Young People's Book Prize, review for the Children's Book Awards, and even perform in the CLiPPA (Centre for Literacy in Primary Poetry Award). Teachers can also shadow shortlists of awards such as the UKLA Book Awards. Engaging in events like these provide exciting opportunities, which children and staff would never normally experience.

Run your own school or smaller-scale class book awards each year to personalise and capitalise on the celebrations for the children. First, let children choose the name of your award. It could be named after your class, your school or something else. Secondly, ask children to decide on different award categories and nominate the books they would like to see in each. The only rules are that they must have read the books if they want to put them forward and be able to explain their reasons why it is a good book. One way of narrowing down the books is to select a shortlist of three to five books for each category, depending on how many you

#BookAwards

have. The categories could be titled 'Best...' or 'Favourite...' and you could award genres like story, non-fiction, poetry, picture book, graphic or other elements such as debuts, read-alouds, book to make you laugh, vilest villain and more. It's up to you and the children!

Once the shortlists have been finalised, alert the authors, illustrators, poets and publishers on social media, congratulating them on being shortlisted, and drum up support for their books. Ask them if they can send your children a personalised message about seeing their book on your shortlists, and share their responses with the children. Display the books around your school and promote the books to staff in book meetings and to your school community through Reading Newsletters **(Idea 76)**, and see if you can purchase multiple copies of the shortlisted book to encourage more children and adults to read them together at once. If a child sees their teacher reading one, I guarantee they'll want to read it! Afterwards, ask children and staff to review them and to vote for their winners.

Finally, host a ceremony to announce the winners. Live-tweet the event using your book award name hashtag so that the authors and illustrators can follow along to find out which books win. If possible, invite them to the ceremony in person or virtually and hand out actual awards.

**Taking it further**

Contact publishers and organisations to put forward your school as a location to host local and national book awards ceremonies, with children and staff involved.

# Rethinking Reading Rewards

"We want to develop a love of reading, rather than the receiving of rewards for reading'.

**Are children reading for the right reasons? Remember that we want children reading for pleasure and not purely for points or prizes. Take time to recognise children's reasons for reading — internalised and externalised — and whether we help or hinder them by reflecting on if and how we reward it.**

Changing the culture of reading rewards in a school can be a challenging task, but it is important for teachers to consider the impact that these rewards can have on children's motivation to read.

We need to be careful that we don't reinforce the message to children that reading is only worth doing for rewards. Certificates, challenges and competitions are not really what reading for pleasure is all about. Every school does things differently, but you should weigh up whether it may be more beneficial to remove or replace reading rewards to guarantee that children develop a real love of reading.

Here are a few tips for changing the culture of reading and rethinking rewards in your school:

1 **Focus on reading for pleasure:** Rather than using rewards as a way to motivate children to read, focus on promoting reading for pleasure and the intrinsic impacts such as the personal growth that can come from engaging with books. Encourage pupils to choose books that interest them and to read for the enjoyment of it, rather than for external rewards.

**#RethinkingReading Rewards**

2 **Rethink reading rewards:** If you still want to reward reading in your school, why not reward it with more reading? Changing the culture of prize-giving to children receiving books as a reward is a significant shift in the right direction. Rather than rewarding individual reading, consider how you can recognise class reading achievements or celebrate the school's overall reading culture.

3 **Provide meaningful feedback on their reading:** This might include sharing reading scrapbooks **(Idea 26)**, having one-on-one discussions with children about their reading, or providing personalised reading recommendations. Give them opportunities to discuss their reading with others too.

4 **Encourage children to set their own reading goals:** Instead of imposing a set of reading goals on pupils, ask them to create their own goals and track their progress. This can help children to feel more invested in their reading and more motivated to read.

**Taking it further**

Involve children in the process of changing the culture of reading rewards by asking for their input and feedback. This can help to ensure that any changes are meaningful and effective.

# Reader Recognition

"A little recognition goes a long way."

**If you wish to reward reading in your school, sometimes the most equitable and effective incentive for children is to celebrate their personal growth, success and status as a reader.**

Many schools have celebration assemblies each week where teachers nominate those who have worked hard, demonstrated positive attitudes to learning, good behaviour or academic achievement.

During these times, teachers could also choose to announce a 'Reading Champion' or 'Reader of the Week' from their class. This is somebody who has set a fantastic example with their reading for a multitude of reasons. They might have been enthusiastic about books and the pleasure of reading, discovered a new author, visited the school or local library in their own time, read lots at home, made good progress with their reading, or read aloud with confidence.

Take a photo of each 'Reading Champion' holding their favourite book for a classroom or school gallery display where other children and staff can add their own congratulatory comments. They could also have other special responsibilities such as visiting other classes to read stories to them, or reading aloud to their own class from the class book.

#ReaderRecognition

# Transition Time

"Supporting transition through books has given children a renewed sense of optimism and enthusiasm."

**Help children at the troublesome time of the school year that is transition with this idea.**

Transitions in primary school are crucial. This includes for children **starting school**, those **moving up** to the next year group or between key stages, and those in their final year **moving on** to secondary school.

**Teaching tip**

Pass on children's reading histories and preferences to their next teacher (or secondary schools).

Sharing books before, during and after transition with themes such as new beginnings, changes and making friends can be a wonderful way to ease this tricky process.

On your transition day(s), start as you mean to go on by reading aloud to your new class, so they see you straight away as a reader teacher. During this day, you could also use a number of reading-related activities such as Reading Surveys **(Idea 6)** to get to know them, as well as planning time for children to explore the reading materials and resources that will be in their new classroom next year.

If you're a Year 6 teacher, liaise with your local secondary schools so that children can have an opportunity to tour their library together with the librarian whilst on their transition visit(s).

**Bonus idea** ★

Talk to your secondary schools to find out if children from feeder primaries could form transition reading groups before attending, or have shared 'transition texts' to read during the holidays to make them feel more connected with their new classmates, as they can talk about it with them in their welcome week in September.

If children recognise books from before by seeing the same authors or series they've started within classroom collections and school libraries in their subsequent year groups or secondary schools, this 'crossover' can be reassuring. Speak to staff in these settings so that literature is overlapped to provide feelings of familiarity and continuity for children to be 'reading-ready' in their new surroundings.

**#TransitionTime**

# Understanding
text types

Part 6

# Fantastic Fiction

"Reading fiction can leave a remarkable and long-lasting impact on children."

**Whether learning about the past, experiencing the present, or imagining the future, here's how you can make the most of it in your classroom.**

Fiction refers to literature that's invented by the imagination. Reading fiction is an important part of a child's reading journey as it plays a major role in expanding their imaginations because children can travel the world through books without leaving their classrooms. Many stories also include moral messages about topics and themes to teach them new things. By reading fiction, children will become more well-rounded individuals with empathy **(Idea 14)**, emotional intelligence and respect for other people.

Children should be reading fiction in your classroom for multiple reasons, such as to be entertained, to be engaged, to be enlightened, to be educated and to empathise.

Like music or movies, children may prefer one kind of fictional book over another, so as a teacher it helps to be aware of the differences between genres and subgenres when selecting books to read aloud or for children to choose to read in your classroom. Examples include: fantasy, funny, magical, mystery, horror, historical fiction, sci-fi, sporting stories, adventure, traditional tales, and film and TV tie-ins.

**#FantasticFiction**

# Face the Facts

"Factual books fuel the fire for furthering children's curiosity."

**Reading often focuses on fiction, with it taking up significant shelf space in schools and dominating book choices. By filling classrooms with factual books too, teachers connect children with the wider world and feed their inborn inquisitive nature so they see reading them as a source of satisfaction.**

Children are naturally and passionately curious with a capital C. You can nurture this by reading and providing a wide range of factual books, including subject-specific reference books, narrative non-fiction biographies, encyclopaedias, newspapers, manuals, blogs, maps, cookbooks, guidebooks, puzzles, quizzes, joke books, activity books and more.

Non-fiction can be a great gateway to reading for pleasure. Written and illustrated by experts in their fields, non-fiction books are factually reliable, relevant and well-researched (unlike some information on the internet) with content pitched and presented appropriately for their intended audiences. Through their varied and visual styles, they highlight the extraordinary in the everyday as well as being a form of escapism and enjoyment, ignite children's interests, inspire awe and wonder, and immerse and invite them into a way of reading that sometimes stories cannot match.

Children also need to learn how to search for and select information, check for accuracy, and question and think critically about the issues facing our society such as considering bias and fake news. Books like these also encourage empathy and children to be at the 'cutting edge' of knowledge, and if we want to provide them with an entirety of reading experiences, we have to value factual books too.

## Teaching tip

Pairing factual with fictional texts provides the perfect complement in the classroom. Some stories also contain appendices that reveal their rich research and historical background so look out for these.

## Taking it further

Celebrate National Non-Fiction November, a month-long reading feast of all things factual, every year.

## Bonus idea ★

Bring in factual as well as fictional writers for your author visits.

**#FaceTheFacts**

# Poetry for Pleasure

"Poetry can be a forgotten area of the curriculum but it has so much potential when it comes to reading for pleasure."

**Create a poetry-for-pleasure classroom where children hear, read, recite, share and see poems in different situations.**

**Teaching tip**

Remember there's no single correct way to write or read poetry, so go your own way with it!

**Taking it further**

Work with professional poets or adopt a 'Patron of Poetry' so children can directly participate in poetry creation, performance and presentation, and get involved in annual poetry awards.

**Bonus idea** ★

Many children's books make use of poetry within them. Read rhyming stories and novels written in verse to introduce children to poetry within literature.

The teaching of poetry has often paled in comparison to other areas of the curriculum. But it's a key form of expression that should be a built-in, not bolted-on, part of all children's educational experiences and your school's environment and ethos. Within poetry there lies a world of possibilities. It's language-rich, open-ended and offers so many opportunities to explore and interpret thoughts, ideas and emotions rather than 'right' answers. It also provides children with another route to reading for pleasure through wordplay, patterns, repetition, rhythm and rhyme (remember they don't always have to rhyme!).

Children need to encounter a wealth of types and forms of poetry from rhymes, riddles, sonnets and songs to limericks, kennings, cinquains, haiku, acrostics, calligrams, concrete and blackout poetry, written by a representative range of classic and contemporary poets from across the world.

Read a poem aloud daily, in the same way that you would do with a chapter of your class book. There are many collections and anthologies available. Or better still, encourage children to sign up to share poems they have chosen from these at times throughout the school day and however they wish to enjoy performing poems without any analysis of them.

**#PoetryForPleasure**

# The Power of Picture Books

"The power and pleasure of picture books in our primary school is palpable."

**A picture is worth a thousand words, and picture books should be shared with children from the youngest to the oldest. Use these ideas to include them as an important part of your reading offer, and to see how they are so much more than simply a stepping stone.**

Do you remember reading the picture books that first brought you pleasure? Or ones that were read to you before you could read? Within them, the illustrations and the words work together to tell the story. Generally, the illustrations are equally as important as, and can be more important than, the words. Usually, they are on every page or each spread (a pair of opposite-facing pages) and these types of books often have a strong, unique concept and a sense of interactivity and re-readability.

Types of picture books you should seek to provide include board books, picture book biographies and wordless picture books. Board books are perfect for putting into the hands of your youngest readers because they are short and withstand wear and tear due to their durability. Picture book biographies introduce the lives of significant people and how they have shaped the world. Wordless picture books encourage children to be creative in their interpretations, as they are told only through illustrations.

When carefully chosen, picture books can also bring inclusivity and diversity into classrooms, acting as a catalyst for starting meaningful conversations about age, gender, race or ethnicity, disability, religion or belief, as well as promoting values such as kindness, honesty, respect and friendship.

**Teaching tip**

Challenge the perception that picture books are only for very young children by creating a culture in which they are enjoyed and appreciated across the school with all year groups.

**Taking it further**

Use picture books as Whole School Books **(Idea 58)** for greater engagement.

**Bonus idea** ★

Give children opportunities to draw their own illustrations in response to reading picture books.

**#ThePowerOf PictureBooks**

# Graphic Novels

"One of my most surprising discoveries this year is seeing how much my class loves graphic novels."

**Graphic novels are an often-underused yet useful reading resource to have in your classroom collections and school library. A welcome change compared to traditional books, they can offer children a different route into discovering the pleasure of reading.**

## Teaching tip

Read a range of graphic novels, such as when reading by example **(Idea 37)**, in your book-based curriculum **(Idea 59)** and choose them as Class Books **(Idea 17)** because they make great read-alouds!

## Taking it further

Start a graphic novel club for children at your school to discover and discuss these texts, and create their own.

Graphic novels are written and illustrated in the style of a comic, which combine short bursts of text with captions, dialogue and vivid illustrations. They usually unfold in a clear sequence, commonly presented in a series of rectangular panels and are also often action-packed and visually stimulating.

The format has seen a recent rise in popularity, meaning that many publishers are producing a range of graphic novels that are high quality and appropriate for all readers. They can be found in a wide assortment of fictional genres: fantasy, science fiction, historical fiction, fairy tales and myths — as well as factual, including biography, history and science.

They are especially appealing to readers who may not be tempted to pick up more traditional books, because of the lively storylines, expressive illustrations and the reduced amount of text on each page. Some graphic novels are also wordless, which encourage readers to look closely at the illustrations and make their own interpretations. They also add an extra layer of support that young readers need to help them through a text with their side-by-side text and illustrations which provide pictorial context.

Encourage graphic novels as part of a varied reading diet for all children in your classroom, so that everyone benefits from this format.

**#GraphicNovels**

# Cultivating
a reading
community

**Part 7**

# Reading Newsletters

"They show all the wonderful ways we promote reading and have been so well-received."

**Share the love of literature through newsletters and inform children, families and staff about everything related to reading happening at school, local, national and international levels.**

Newsletters could be produced termly, half termly or monthly to update your school community on reading and sustain a reading relationship between school and home. They could include the following features:

- a focus on an author or illustrator
- a welcome page with a personalised message/Q&A from an author or illustrator
- school or local library opening times
- information on local independent bookshops
- books that year groups are reading in class
- staff recommendations of children's books
- special themed editions covering different genres, topics, events, celebrations, etc.
- what the school's Book Club is reading **(Idea 63)**, their recommendations and reviews
- a space for the Reading Representatives **(Idea 55)** to share how they influence reading in the school from a pupil perspective
- interviews with children, staff and families as reading role models about their preferences
- recommendations of books for parents
- details of reading events and competitions
- reports and round-ups of any reading-related activities in school or the local area
- top tips, inspiration, resources and reminders

Newsletters should be available in classrooms and across the school; for all children, teaching and support staff, senior leadership and governors; and sent out via the school's website, social media and communication channels for families and the wider community.

**#Reading Newsletters**

# School Socials

"Our school social media account and hashtag really reinforces our love of reading."

**Create connections with your wider community using your own school social media account and reading-related hashtag to promote reading for pleasure.**

Social media has its critics but used well, the strengths of it in transforming your school into a reading school shouldn't be underestimated. Using social media in school is more effective if it has a clear purpose so why not create specific accounts for celebrating and sharing reading for pleasure?

**Teaching tip**

Before posting, always ensure that parental permissions and consent have been sought for photos of children to appear on social media.

Decide on the platforms to use. Are these ones that staff are familiar with and that most parents use? Agree if the pages will be public or whether access must be requested, whether parents can post to the page and reply to others, or if comments will be turned off. Remind families of the correct procedures for raising concerns in your school, which shouldn't be done online. It is also advisable to have a code of conduct for everyone setting out the expectations for appropriate behaviour.

**Taking it further**

For extra engagement, your school's posts could be shown repeatedly rolling on screens around your school to make reading visible **(Idea 91)**.

Next, create your own personalised reading-related account handle and/or hashtag for your school. This could be by adding the word 'Reads' or 'Reading' or the letters 'RfP' for Reading for Pleasure to the end of your school name. Ask staff and families to tag your handle and tweet your hashtag in their posts and pictures to share everything associated with reading they are doing in school and at home so that everyone across the school can see them. Make sure to consider which members of staff will be posting and responding regularly on your school socials and if they have the capacity or time to do so.

**#SchoolSocials**

# Reading Volunteers

"Our volunteers play a vital role in sustaining our reading culture."

**Recruit a team of trusted volunteers to support your school by spending time regularly reading with children, developing reading relationships and making a real and rewarding difference.**

A reading volunteer scheme involves members of your local community signing up to listen to children read, read to them and talk to them about their reading. Almost anyone can do it. Your team could comprise families, governors and others, such as trainee teachers from universities and students from secondary schools, which helps to strengthen local links.

Reading volunteers could help in a range of situations including reading to whole classes, with groups, or on a one-to-one basis. For safeguarding, ensure that enhanced DBS (Disclosure and Barring Service) checks are carried out for all volunteers, and they know about policies and procedures.

They will require initial training to get them started so run sessions to support them to provide this type of service effectively.

You could share set structures for them to work with children, such as this four-part format:

- **Recap:** what has happened in the book so far or if new, make predictions
- **Read:** listen, check understanding and support vocabulary as children read to them
- **Reflect:** discuss the book, ask questions and share opinions and preferences together
- **Record:** record with the child what's been read so that staff and parents can see

By having reading volunteers and them taking the time to volunteer, your school is showing how important it is for everyone to read.

# Community Collaboration

"Collaborating with our community makes us feel better connected and shows we care for others."

**Strong communities benefit schools and they have a proactive part to play in this outreach. Here's some steps that teachers and schools can do to work together to give back to them.**

A school is a community in its own right. But when you extend that to the wider community, the benefits for everyone can be significant, especially when it comes to reading.

Schools should aim to build reading relationships within their wider communities, in ways that work for them, such as:
- creating community libraries by converting unused places for people to exchange books, e.g. phone boxes;
- designing community reading areas and spaces, e.g. reading benches or gardens;
- reading to and with people in the community, e.g. to residents at care homes;
- making reading visible in your community, e.g. book trails and window sharing;
- donating books, e.g. being 'Book Fairies' and hiding books in public for others to find;
- working with local libraries, e.g. selecting new stock for their children's section;
- supporting local bookshops with shared initiatives, e.g. book fairs or wishlists;
- organising and/or offering school facilities, e.g. for adult literacy classes for local people;
- campaigning with local companies, e.g. to encourage their customers to read;
- collaborating with colleges or universities, e.g. working with trainee teachers;
- partnering with national and international organisations, e.g. on large-scale programmes.

**Teaching tip**

If you're new to your school or don't know the area, maximise the connections that the children and their families already have.

**Taking it further**

Identify where children spend time out-of-school and collaborate with community services to bring books to places such as hairdressers, doctors' and dentists' waiting rooms, hospitals, supermarkets, foodbanks, sports stadiums and community centres.

**Bonus idea** ★

You could suggest children's books reviews or recommendations or show what you're doing with reading as a school by writing in your local newspaper or shout out about books by broadcasting on a school radio station.

**#Community Collaboration**

# Festival Friends

"We've been bringing children to our local literature festival for many years, and we hope to do so for many more!"

**Nurture the next generation of readers and enliven the experience for your school's budding bookworms by taking them to a literary festival on site or online.**

**Taking it further**

Many festivals are very family friendly so share events with families through your communication channels and school socials to encourage them to attend.

There are growing numbers of children's literary festivals for book lovers of all ages, from preschool to primary, happening every year across the country. But for many children, these are opportunities that are out of reach and they are unlikely to attend due to distance, cost or other reasons.

Most festivals run designated, extensive and free primary school programmes, with some also offering funding in the form of grants and bursaries to cover costs. So why not enable children to enjoy a new, inclusive and unforgettable event they might not otherwise experience, by taking them along to see a line-up of live literature at a literary festival?

From readings and signings to interactive sessions and creative workshops, children can come face-to-face with their favourite authors and illustrators. If it's successful, you could take children every year as one of your annual trips so that every child has a chance to visit during their time at your school.

**Bonus idea** ★

As part of their outreach programmes some festivals offer 'Schools Weeks', where authors and illustrators visit nearby schools to lead activities – so look out for these opportunities!

If you can't attend in person, many festivals across the world also make their programmes available digitally so you can access events to watch live on the day or on catch-up, bringing books to life in your school or even to children learning from home at a time that suits you. Some events will also be accompanied by teaching materials produced by the festivals, to support and encourage further learning.

# Book Fair

"They are instrumental in introducing so many different books to children."

**Book fair week is an exciting time for everyone! Not only do they help to fuel a love of reading but hosting them is also a great way to support your school's reading efforts.**

Book fairs can be a great way to bring the school community together. They can help spark a love of reading across the school by introducing children, parents and staff to a wide range of books and authors. They can browse through different genres and find books that interest them, which can encourage them to develop a lifelong love of reading.

Many also serve as fundraisers for schools. Schools can use the funds raised to purchase new books for classroom collections, the school library or invest in other resources that support literacy and learning.

Many retailers will run the fair for you, including setting up, staffing, selling, handling money and clearing away, as well as providing pre-fair planning visits and after-fair advice. All you'll need to provide is a shared space like your school's hall or library.

Schedule 'sneak-peeks' for children to come in with their class earlier in the day to get a better look at the books without it being too busy, or 'show and tell' sessions from the bookseller to visit classes to talk about the books on offer beforehand. All children should be able to see the selections available throughout the day, such as at break and lunch times, and you could open it before and after school.

**Taking it further**

Ensure book fairs coincide with parents' evenings, open doors afternoons or other school events to encourage maximum engagement.

**Bonus idea** ★

Could you choose to work with your local independent bookshop to provide a bespoke book fair for your school, as well as show your support for small businesses?

**#BookFair**

# Fundraising and Finance

"Thanks to the fundraising of our school community, we now have so many new books and are planning to take our children to a literary festival, as well as invite authors in."

**As anyone who works in a school knows, funding is a constant challenge because there are always expenses that need to be covered. One area that is often underfunded is the school library, and this can make it difficult for schools to purchase new books and maintain a well-stocked library. Here are some sources and strategies that schools can use to finance the purchase of books.**

**Teaching tip**

Use your School Socials **(Idea 77)** to enter giveaways and competitions on social media from authors, publishers and other organisations to win free books, author visits **(Idea 98)** or virtual visits **(Idea 100)**.

Schools can raise money for books through grants and donations. Many organisations, both public and private, offer grants specifically for educational purposes, including the purchase of books. Schools can research these grant opportunities and apply for funding. Many are happy to support education such as the Foyle Foundation and the Siobhan Dowd Trust, and by making a compelling case for the need for new books in their proposals, schools can often secure donations. Additionally, schools can reach out to companies, councils, and charitable and community organisations to ask for donations. Some supermarkets also have their own schemes to help schools.

Another way that schools can raise funds for books is through fundraisers. There are many different types of fundraisers that schools can hold, from bake sales and car washes to silent auctions and raffles. If you have a Parent Teacher Association, you could also work with them to raise money, with profits from stalls at summer fetes, sports days, parents' evenings or festivals of reading **(Idea 83)** going towards purchasing books. By getting creative and involving the whole school community, schools can often raise a significant amount of money through fundraisers.

**#Fundraising AndFinance**

In addition to raising funds through grants, donations and fundraisers, schools can also look for other sources of financing. For example, some schools have formed partnerships with bookstores or publishers to purchase books at a discounted rate. They can use the proceeds from book fairs **(Idea 81)** or other book sales to purchase new books. You could also consider crowdfunding and sponsored events.

Shadowing and judging book awards is another way to receive books, as are contacting organisations who send free copies to schools to read in exchange for reviews from children and teachers. Children could run their own enterprise projects to raise funds for books for your school or to donate to another organisation that you have links with. You could also hold a book drive **(Idea 84)** where you sell pre-loved books from the school stock and donations from the community at a reduced price to raise funds.

**Taking it further**

Set up a wishlist of books you would like to buy for your school with your local bookshop or an online retailer. Share a link to this with your school community for people to know what you need to complete your collections.

# Festival of Reading

"Last year was the first time we held our Festival of Reading, and it was such a roaring success for everyone in our school. We'll definitely be doing it again next year!"

**Arrange an annual whole school event to make connections with your community by building reading relationships and showcasing your school's successful love of reading.**

Imagine the impact of holding your own Festival of Reading: a special event to promote literacy and a love of reading, and celebrate all the school's hard work and progress on raising the profile of reading throughout the year. Sounds incredible, right?

Organising a Festival of Reading can seem daunting, but with careful planning and the help of the community, schools can successfully host their own celebration of literature.

Here are some steps that schools can follow for running their own Festival of Reading:

**Allocate funds:** Check that there are approved funds available to start the planning process of your whole school reading festival.

**Set a date:** Choose a date that works for the school and the community. Consider factors such as school schedules and the availability of volunteers. It could be an alternative to your traditional Summer Fayre.

**Plan the event:** Decide on the details, including the format, locations and programme. Some ideas for activities could include: author and illustrator workshops; book sales, swaps and signings; storytelling sessions and creative reading-related activities; fundraising; live music; and food, drink and entertainment stalls.

**Book your guests:** Consider a range of creators to provide representation (**Idea 60**).

**#FestivalOfReading**

Usually, they are snapped up well in advance, particularly around World Book Day, so be aware of booking them ahead of schedule. Try to ensure that children will have read at least one of their books by the time they visit so that they are familiar with them.

**Promote the event:** To ensure it's well-attended, it's important to promote the event to the community. This can include sharing information about the event on your school socials and communication channels, sending out flyers, and reaching out to media outlets to publicise the event on local and national levels.

**Invite the community:** Encourage children, parents, staff and community members to attend.

**Seek sponsors and donations:** Contact local businesses and organisations to seek sponsorships or donations for the event. This can help offset the costs of hosting and provide additional resources for activities and prizes.

**Prepare materials and resources:** Gather the necessary materials and resources for the event, including books, decorations and supplies in advance.

**Involve children:** Children can participate in activities during the reading festival, promote it by creating flyers and posters to generate excitement and increase attendance, and assist with setting up, decorating and cleaning up the event space before and after it.

**Coordinate with local bookshops or libraries:** Partner with local bookstores or libraries to provide the opportunities to buy and borrow books at the festival, as well as raise awareness about events like the Summer Reading Challenge **(Idea 88)**.

**Execute the event:** On the day of the Festival of Reading, it's important to ensure that everything runs smoothly. This can include setting up tables and chairs, providing refreshments and coordinating any special events or activities.

> **Bonus idea** ★
>
> Open your festival to families and the local community on the weekend to maximise attendance levels but consider the capacity, workload and wellbeing of staff if you choose to do so.

# Drives and Donation Schemes

"Gifting books is the greatest gesture of all."

**As a child, the effects of owning a book can be revolutionary: make sure all the children in your school get to bring home books, even if they can't buy them.**

**Taking it further**

Dedicate shelves in your school where second-hand books in good condition can be donated, swapped over and given to parents and children for free. Not only does this promote environmental awareness through the reusing of books but it's also an act of kindness.

Many children will read books regularly and visit local libraries and bookshops, but think about those that don't own a single book of their own at home. There is a considerable imbalance in access to reading as that's the reality for hundreds of thousands of children growing up today, and some will be sitting in your classroom or school.

Organising book drives and donation schemes can be an effective way for schools to increase the number of books available to children. This is when your school community can bring in any children's books that they no longer need, and they can be given away freely to all children. Set up collection points at the school and in the community, such as at local libraries, bookshops or shops in city and town centres to make it easier for people to donate.

Running whole school book swap events can also be a great way to provide greater access to reading, where children can exchange gently-used books for new-to-them ones.

There are also local, national and international charities and campaigns who provide free books to schools. These include Bookstart, Book Buddy, the Marcus Rashford Book Club and Puffin's World of Stories. You may even have your own community book gifting schemes available in your area too.

**#DrivesAndDonation Schemes**

# Love your libraries

# Part 8

# School Library

"Our library is the beacon, bedrock and beating heart of our school."

**Every child deserves a great school library because they play such a pivotal role in reading and can make the ultimate difference in developing your reading culture.**

**Taking it further**

Send selections of brand new books on a tour of your school to spend a day in each class, before putting them into the school library.

Here are some things to consider when setting up a school library, especially if it's entirely new:

1 **Set up a steering group:** Include staff and children to plan out your school library.
2 **Draw up a development and action plan:** This helps to consider the costs of resourcing, replenishing or refurbishing.
3 **Consult your school community:** Ask them questions on what they want from the library and use their answers to inform your plans.
4 **Choose a location:** Make sure it is easily accessible and convenient for children and staff. Consider factors such as proximity to classrooms, natural light and size.
5 **Select and organise stock:** Consider a range of books to appeal to children of all ages and interests including fiction, non-fiction, poetry, picture books and graphic novels. Organise them by age group, author or genre so it's easy for children to find what they want.
6 **Choose furniture and shelving:** Ensure it's appropriate for the library's size. Offer a range of comfortable seating and tables for children to use while reading on their own or together.
7 **Set up a circulation system:** Set up a system for checking out and returning books. Consider employing a qualified school librarian to manage and assist children.
8 **Promote the library:** Encourage pupils to visit and use it to host events, such as book clubs or author visits. Consider setting up displays to encourage children to explore the library.

**Bonus idea** ★

Make available an adults' selection area of books in your school library for parents.

**#SchoolLibrary**

# School Librarian

"School librarians shouldn't be underrated but be statutory and specifically funded in our schools."

**If your school is fortunate enough to have its own school librarian, you'll already know that you have someone who is of significant value to your children and staff. But if you don't, you should try everything possible to employ them, as a library without a librarian is lacking in more ways than one.**

Without question, one of the most important members of staff you can have in your school is a school librarian because they are a driving force for developing reading for pleasure.

School librarians are trained professionals who have specialist knowledge about a wide range of literature and can help children to find books appropriate to their age and interests. They also provide invaluable experience and expertise in knowing what children are regularly reading which can be worthwhile for teachers with limited knowledge of children's literature.

School librarians can also encourage children to discover new authors and genres. By providing recommendations and highlighting new releases, they can help children to explore different styles of literature and broaden their horizons. This can help children develop a more diverse reading palate and encourage a deeper love of reading. They also make books accessible through running library lessons and reading groups in their libraries, which act as safe shared spaces for the school community.

If money doesn't allow your school to employ a full-time librarian, consider the options of recruiting a part-time school librarian, sharing librarians across local schools, and working closely together with your schools' library service — if you are lucky enough to have one.

**Taking it further**

School librarians can train children to take on different responsibilities in the running of the school library so they can learn new skills which they can take back and use in their classroom collections.

**Bonus idea** ★

Could librarians from your local library also regularly visit your school to complement the services of your school librarian?

**#SchoolLibrarian**

**IDEA 87**

# Local Library

"The realisation that children could borrow books for free, whenever they wanted, was groundbreaking for them!"

**Make good use of your local library with this community-centred idea...**

Libraries are life-changing for children and part of a community's lifeblood. But their long-term future is under threat from years of funding cuts, leading to closures across the country. It's more important than ever not to take the ones we still have for granted; many face the ultimatum of us using them or losing them.

Whether your local library is in walking distance or a short bus ride away, schedule regular times for children to visit. This could be to browse and borrow books, learn more about what the library provides from the library staff, or to participate in events. Plan a whole school programme so that each class can visit ideally at least once per term (at least three visits a year).

Schools can also work with local libraries to:

- utilise their resources, such as electronic databases or e-books, to supplement the school's own library collection;
- host book clubs or bring in authors for visits;
- work together to encourage reading by participating in initiatives, such as inviting librarians into school to talk about the Summer Reading Challenge.

Make children and their families aware that alongside print books, libraries provide services such as: free internet access; printing, copying and scanning; music and film rental; ebooks and audiobooks; family history research access; storytime sessions for preschool children; technological assistance; skills courses; community groups; and council services.

**Teaching tip**

Sign up for 'class cards' from your local library which will allow teachers to have extended loans.

**Taking it further**

Encourage every child to be a member of the local library by sending out joining forms to families.

**Bonus idea** ★

Invite local librarians to stop by the school regularly, perhaps during parents' evenings or after school, to encourage families to sign up by showing them the services on offer and bringing samples of books.

#LocalLibrary

108

# Summer Reading Challenge

"A fantastic way to keep children reading through the summer holidays!"

**Getting children to read over the summer can be a challenge, so collaborate with local libraries on their fun, free six-week solution to stop the summer slump and strengthen a love of reading.**

The Summer Reading Challenge is produced by The Reading Agency and takes place nationally every year in local libraries during the summer holidays, supporting children to continue reading for pleasure over the six-week break. Each year, the Challenge motivates over 700,000 children to keep reading by having a different theme that sparks children's curiosity about the world around them.

The Challenge encourages family engagement and involvement in reading and helps your school make links with the library and the wider community. It can also be the start of a child's reading journey and prevents the tendency for children's reading to dip over the holidays.

It's open to all primary school children. You can promote it to children and parents by using your school socials and communication channels to send out information about it and how to get involved for free at a participating library. The aim is for children to borrow six library books or more. They receive special stickers and rewards each time they finish a book. There's also a certificate and a medal for everyone who completes the Challenge, and there are bigger prize draws too!

Children can read whatever they like in their chosen format. Those who take part become more enthusiastic about reading, return to school keen and ready to read in September, and boost their confidence and self-esteem.

**Teaching tip**

Invite local librarians in to talk about the Summer Reading Challenge before the summer holidays, and afterwards to award certificates.

**#SummerReading Challenge**

# Engaging with your reading environment

**Part 9**

# Door Displays

"Our door displays help reading to be seen and talked about so much more often."

**Inspire an infectious buzz about books with this idea to help you use the space available, get the balance right and showcase reading right across your school.**

Classroom doors are used every day – they're passed often on the way to the hall, playground and other communal areas, and they're the first focal point of your classroom. Make reading visible **(Idea 91)** around your school by displaying what classes are reading on the doors of their classrooms.

You could include a sign which signposts what Class Book **(Idea 17)** you are reading, images of those your class have previously read to record their year's reading and what they are wanting to read next. Change this regularly throughout the year so everyone sees each class as a community of readers.

Likewise, encourage teachers to display what they are reading on their doors too. Staff could show children that they read books aimed at adults as well as children. Try to include a mix of fiction and non-fiction, including newspapers, magazines, audiobooks and any appropriate reading material. If staff have their own children, they could also include what they are reading to their children at home.

#DoorDisplays

# Front-Facing

"The power of a front-facing book is incredible. They stand out so much to the children!"

**Children care more about seeing the cover of a book than its spine, so use these simple shelving strategies to help them to search more successfully and promote the plentiful picking up of books in your classroom easily and at eye-level.**

Front-facing books make choosing a book easier for children because they are attractive, attention-grabbing and they can easily see what's available. So what are you waiting for? Step away from your shelves to take a look at them and re-evaluate whether they're working for readers.

There are several ways in which you can display front-facing books in your classroom to make them easily accessible to children. One option is to use low shelves bookcases and window sills that allow children to easily browse and select books on their own. You can also use book baskets placed at child height, so that children can easily see and reach the books inside. Another way is to use a book carousel or rotating book display, which allows children to spin the display and see all the available books at once. At least one of the displays you have in your classroom should be front-facing only.

No matter how you choose to display front-facing books in your classroom, it is important to make sure that the books are located and organised in a way that is easy for children to navigate. This might mean grouping books by genre, or using labels or other visual aids to help children find the books they're looking for.

**Teaching tip**

Rotate your front-facing books regularly to refresh them – make it the children's decision which books get that pride of place every time you do so.

**Bonus idea** ★

Repurpose storage solutions like spice, plate and toast racks or hanging shoe compartments for front-facing displays at an affordable cost.

**#FrontFacing**

# Make Reading Visible

"We see, hear and feel reading right the way through our school."

**Targeting these three essential environments will ensure that children see that reading is all around us.**

From classrooms to corridors, walls to windows, the staffroom to the school library, and the hall to the headteacher's office, how do you communicate to your school community that reading is important **inside** your school?

Is your reading culture reflected in the physical environment through a range of reading places and spaces **(Idea 92)**? If someone stood somewhere in your school, what would they see and what would it say about attitudes and approaches to reading? Do you also positively present, permit and promote reading for pleasure through adults and children's choices?

What about **outside**? Is reading shown on the exterior to the same extent as in the interior? Think about reading as a thread that runs throughout your school, and think outside the bricks of your building. Are there opportunities for reading to occur outside? Do children and staff regularly read and talk about books in the playground: at breaktime, lunchtime and during the day? Is reading depicted in larger-than-life displays or murals of books and characters in your school's surroundings?

Visibility extends to your **online** environment, such as your school's website, social media and other communication channels. How can you connect with your community? How does reading for pleasure in your school look from the perspective of a parent or visitor?

Evaluating the experiences you provide will help to create a sustained and successful reading-rich environment for everyone.

**#MakeReading Visible**

# Reading Places and Spaces

"The more places and spaces schools have to read, the more children will be motivated to read anywhere and everywhere."

**Places and spaces are at a premium in primary schools, but think about how you can spice and spruce things up to use every spare centimetre creatively to encourage a zest for reading.**

Classrooms and school libraries will usually be the predominant reading places, but go beyond those to provide many spaces for relaxed and recreational reading across the building.

Some places and spaces you can create to give children opportunities to read include:

- **Reading nooks:** Designate specific spaces to have comfortable seating and plenty of books where children can go to relax and read, either individually or in small groups. Specifying noise levels with loud, quiet and silent areas can also make huge differences.
- **Circulation zones:** These are perhaps some of the busiest sites so think about how book vending machines, murals, displays and shelving can create 'reading corridors'.
- **School halls:** Consider how these multi-functional areas can promote reading, with displays and Reading Assemblies **(Idea 56)**.
- **Stairwells:** These are innovative places to promote reading; try installing reading-related illustrations such as staircase riser graphics showing large book spines to stimulate children's visual senses and talk.
- **Outdoor reading areas:** Consider creating outdoor spaces dedicated to reading, such as simple spots with a bench or picnic table; more elaborate areas with a Storytellers' Chair, log circles, little libraries and book exchange boxes; or outdoor classrooms and reading sheds with comfortable seating and shade where children can read all year round.

**Taking it further**

Tour your school and take photos of where reading happens. Go beyond the obvious and think about possible new places for reading too.

**#ReadingPlaces AndSpaces**

# Participating with parents and families

**Part 10**

# Parent Partners

"If schools and parents work together to encourage reading, it pays off big time for both parties."

**Get parents and families actively involved to increase interest and investment, and sustain your home–school reading relationships.**

Family engagement in reading is fundamental. Since not all of them recognise the importance of their roles or have the resources to do so, schools should be doing everything possible to provide a positive partnership with parents.

Schools can provide times for families to talk to teachers about their children's reading habits at home and understand their children's reading in school through parents' evenings **(Idea 94)**, reports **(Idea 95)** and Reading Workshops **(Idea 96)**.

Host reading events as a fun and social way for families to connect over books and reading at your school. These could be 'open doors' opportunities during the day to visit your school to read with their children, as well as chances for them to volunteer to read with other children.

Share lists of recommended books, websites and other reading resources with parents so that they can support their children's reading at home. Consider creating your own school-selected recommended reading lists or newsletters that include suggestions of books for different age groups and interests.

Create community book clubs and places for parents to pick up a book such as book swap shelves in your school, as well as book fairs at parents' evenings and invite them to come with you when visiting your local libraries or literary festivals **(Idea 80)**.

**#ParentPartners**

# Parents' Evenings

"There isn't a more perfect chance to come together, chat about and celebrate children's reading for pleasure both in the classroom and at home."

**Throughout the school year, the opportunities to meet personally with parents can sometimes seem to be few and far between. But parents' evenings can offer the optimal place for reflection about reading for pleasure to occur and for you to learn about their home-habits and reading role models.**

It's important that teachers take advantage of the time together at every parents' evening to ensure that reading for pleasure is a central topic of your conversations with families.

Discussing reading for pleasure can highlight the value of it to parents beyond its role in academic achievement. It can also identify any potential challenges or barriers to reading that children may be facing. For example, parents may not be aware of the kinds of books or authors that their children are interested in, or they may not know how to support their children's reading at home. By talking about these, teachers can provide parents with valuable insights, suggestions and strategies for encouraging their children to read more. Having a record of this information from Reading Surveys **(Idea 6)** can help you to drop these details naturally into discussions.

Chatting about reading at parents' evenings can also be an opportunity to celebrate and recognise children's progress and accomplishments in reading. By sharing examples of the books that they are reading and the progress they are making, teachers can help to build a sense of pride and accomplishment and encourage parents to support their children's reading efforts.

**Taking it further**

Ask children to set up a representative range of children's books you read in your school for parents to peruse while they wait for their appointments. This could be in the style of a Pupil to Peer promotion area **(Idea 22)** with children's own reviews and recommendations attached.

**Bonus idea** ★

**Provide opportunities for parents to buy and borrow books and attend reading-related presentations at parents' evenings.**

**#ParentsEvenings**

# Report On Reading

"Parents always comment really positively on how they love hearing about reading in their children's reports, and about the time we've taken to do so."

**Make references to reading in children's annual school reports to help them and their parents understand how they've personally grown and shown that they are a reader.**

### Teaching tip

Before writing, provide children with a Reading Survey **(Idea 6)** asking them about the titles of books they've read, experiences they've enjoyed and other reading-related memories from the past year to include in your reports. This acts not only as a reminder but also adds an extra personal touch. Some responses might surprise you.

### Taking it further

Reports are often received only once in the summer term so think about how you can report on reading for pleasure in real-time in the classroom throughout the year. Can you use technology to do this?

In their reports, do you discuss not just children's reading levels and assessments as required but also aspects of their reading for pleasure, such as their attitudes and achievements?

When writing children's reports, refer explicitly to the titles of books and names of authors and illustrators that children have enjoyed reading throughout the year, and their reasons for liking them. This could be discussed in the 'English' section or 'Reading' subsection of the report, as well as giving examples in the personal comments of how they've demonstrated and developed as a reader.

By including this level of information about children's reading habits, teachers can provide a more complete picture of children's development and help parents to understand the role that reading plays in their children's overall development and make suggestions of books that they can borrow or buy to help their children to continue reading for pleasure.

**#ReportOnReading**

# Reading Workshops

"Reading workshops are a great way to grow as a reading school and community."

**Offer regular reading workshops to involve and invest families in developing their understanding of the teaching and learning of reading, and ensure that your school's reading culture extends into each of their homes.**

By inviting parents to participate in these, schools can encourage collaboration and build a shared understanding of the importance of reading. They can help families to feel more familiar with understanding how their children are learning to read in the classroom, your reading for pleasure culture and how they can get involved and help their children at home.

Provide parents with information about the reading instruction that is taking place in the classroom, including the strategies and approaches that are being used to teach reading such as phonics programmes and reading schemes. Look at examples of books used in your school, and share suggestions where to find recommended books, websites and other reading resources. You could also invite your local library **(Idea 87)**, schools' library service, or bookshops in to showcase a selection.

Reading workshops could take place during the school day or afterwards. They could be held for individual year groups, key stages, or for the whole school; for parents only; or for paired/shared attendance for parent(s) and children to come together depending on their desired purpose.

**Teaching tip**

Provide handouts at the end to cover the main points and helpful tips for people to take away.

**Taking it further**

For maximum engagement, share any presentations from the workshops on your website, communication channels and School Socials **(Idea 77)** for families to access them in their own time. Reading workshops could also be held virtually if necessary.

**Bonus idea** ★

During the workshop, collect feedback from parents and families about: the main reasons for attending; how confident they felt about supporting their children with reading before and after it; what they enjoyed; and any follow-ups for next time, to help you plan future workshops.

**#ReadingWorkshops**

# Working with writers and illustrators

## Part 11

# Author of the Month

"It isn't long before the books on our Author of the Month displays disappear into children's hands."

**Open the eyes of children and staff to the breadth and depth of the writing world and raise their awareness of different authors through a designated display to shine a spotlight on them.**

**Teaching tip**

As children begin to become more confident, ask them to choose the next 'Author of the Month'. Once they've made suggestions, take a vote to decide by Children's Choice **(Idea 1)**.

When asking children or teachers about their favourite authors, are you answered with the usual suspects? Do they have a dependence on Dahl, Donaldson or Dick King-Smith, mention a majority of Morpurgo, or have they become Rowling-reliant? Does it leave you wanting to wean some of them off saying Walliams, Wilson or Wimpy Kid every time?

That's not to say that these are not good to read but celebrities, popular authors and series with film adaptations have become big and extremely marketable in children's literature, with larger advertising budgets behind them. However, in order to expand children's reading horizons we should try to resist solely having books in school that children are most likely to buy or be bought, access at home or see on the supermarket shelves. We also need to be careful that we don't only celebrate the same small number of authors we ourselves read as children.

One way of widening children's reading repertoires and range of authors is by designing 'Author of the Month' displays in your classroom or in a shared space such as your school library, corridor or entrance foyer. An 'Author of the Month' is a specific author who you choose to focus children's attention on.

An array of items can be attached to your 'Author of the Month' display to complement it, including:

**#AuthorOf TheMonth**

- images, information about the author, and any communication with them;
- physical copies of the authors' books to pick up, peruse and read;
- posters of front covers, blurbs and inside elements like maps or illustrations;
- character cut-outs, scenes of settings, quotes, artefacts and any other materials;
- QR codes to videos of the author reading their books;
- reviews of the author's books, as well as those written by the children;
- 'ask the author' questions written by the children to send to the author;
- a countdown chart to the date that their next book is being published, if applicable.

**Taking it further**

Adapt the concept to 'Creator of the Month' by including illustrators and poets to really deepen readers' repertoires.

Change the choice of author each month to expose children to the work of different writers; it could be selected by you or the children. Ensure to include a diverse variety of authors when choosing your 'Author of the Month' in relation to age, disability, gender, race and period they wrote in. Through these, children could be introduced to at least ten authors over the course of a school year. Display a classroom 'Author of the Month' Hall of Fame showing the previous authors' photos so children can refer back to them when choosing their books from classroom collections and the school library.

Dedicate time to talk about your 'Author of the Month' and to read their books with your class. You could also set aside slots for children to research them, and communicate with them to let them know that they are your chosen author and send them some questions to answer. Authors are often very receptive and some may send on display materials to your school.

Share your 'Author of the Month' displays with your wider community. Promote your 'Authors of the Month' across your school in Reading Assemblies **(Idea 56)** and Reading Newsletters **(Idea 76)**, as well as in the school library so that children are able to borrow copies of their books.

# Author Visits

"Author visits have had an immeasurable impact on everyone."

**Meeting authors in real life can be such an especially motivating and memorable experience for children, but they require careful planning, preparation and review to ensure that they are successful. Here are a few things that schools need to consider to make the most out of them.**

Before you begin planning the visit, it is important to determine the goals of the visit and how it will fit into the overall curriculum or reading for pleasure programme at your school.

Next, research and select an author who is appropriate for the age and interests of your children and who aligns with the books you're reading or what you're teaching. Consider reaching out to authors directly or contacting an author agency or publisher to inquire about availability. Demand is particularly high around World Book Day, but children should see authors visiting your school all year round.

Once you have selected an author, work with them to **plan** the details of the visit, including the length of the visit, the format of the presentation and any special requests or needs. Consider the logistical requirements of the visit, such as transportation, accommodation and catering. Check with your author that they have all the information they need in advance, such as contact details and directions to your school, start and finish times, and anything else necessary.

Promote the visit to children, teachers and parents to create excitement and encourage participation. Use your school socials, communication channels, website and posters to spread the word.

**#AuthorVisits**

In the lead-up to the visit, **prepare** children for the event by reading their books, giving them background information about the author and their work, and encourage them to think of questions they would like to ask the author. Contact your local bookshop for help with organisation and sales if necessary.

On the day of the visit, be flexible. Meet and greet your author when they arrive. Make them feel welcome with signing in, meeting staff, showing them key places around the school, and of course time for a cup of tea or coffee. Help them set up any presentations and technology they require, and introduce the author to the children. Oversee the events of the visit to keep them running smoothly, assisting where needed, thanking the author at the end of their events, and supervising signings.

After the visit, send a thank you to the author and pay them promptly. Take the time to **review** the visit and gather feedback from children, teachers and the author. Use this feedback to identify any areas for improvement and to plan for future author visits.

Even though this idea is entitled 'Author Visits', invite illustrators and poets (as well as publishers, editors, booksellers and other industry professionals) to visit your school, so that children see the value of all creators in the publishing process.

Virtual visits **(Idea 100)** are also an alternative to in-person author visits.

# Adopt An Author

"Affording children with opportunities to work with authors has been such a boost for them."

**Build lasting connections between those who create books and the children they create them for.**

Working with authors can provide a sense of engagement and excitement for children as they learn about the author's writing process and hear more about the stories and characters the author has created. It can also inspire writing, performances and other activities. Here are two tried-and-tested ways to do this.

**Patron of Reading** is a scheme for schools to have their own designated children's author, illustrator or poet, with whom they develop a deeper relationship over time. Everything the patron does is centred on building a reading for pleasure culture in the school. This could be through visits, donating their books, involvement in newsletters, giving out awards, contributing to the curriculum and more. The possibilities are virtually endless as each partnership will be different. Created by headteacher Tim Redgrave, see more about the success of the scheme and the range of patrons available at www.patronofreading.co.uk.

**BookPenPals**, founded by Kate Scott and Sara O'Connor, is another initiative that partners UK schools with UK authors and illustrators to act as reading advocates by sending regular book recommendations, advice and tips to classes via postcards, over the course of a school year. Schools reply with their own postcards, either sending recommendations back or giving updates on reading. In some cases, the relationship leads to an in-person or virtual visit. Find out more at www.bookpenpals.com.

> **Bonus idea** ★
>
> Name different classrooms, year groups, class groups or houses in your school after authors and illustrators so children recognise and connect with them, as well as give them greater recognition. Children could contact them to communicate, and invite them to the school to collaborate.

**#AdoptAnAuthor**

# Virtual Visits

"Virtual visits mean that no one misses out on the magic of seeing an author."

**Most authors now offer virtual visits if an in-person visit isn't a viable option, so take up this technological opportunity to see and speak to authors on-screen in your school.**

Virtual visits are online events with an author and classes, year groups or the whole school, streamed via videoconferencing platforms. While a virtual visit may not be able to beat a real-life author visit **(Idea 98)**, it can still bring its own benefits such as: convenience; availability of authors you might not meet otherwise including those who are international; and greater accessibility for schools in rural or remote areas, or which have limited resources.

The process is very similar to scheduling an author visit to your school, however there are also some distinct differences:

1 **What will the virtual visit entail?** There are a variety of online options including presentations, Q&As and even writing stories together. Work with the author to plan the details of the visit.
2 **Consider the technical requirements of the visit:** This includes the types of platform, equipment or software that will be needed. Do you want it to be live, pre-recorded, or a blend of both?
3 **Will there be chances for the children to engage with the author?** If so, in the lead-up to the visit, prepare children for the event by giving them background information about the author and their work and encourage them to think of questions they would like to ask the author. Will the author also provide activities for the children to complete during the event?

**#VirtualVisits**

# Appendix: Whole School Books (Idea 58)

## Anthology
*The Book of Hopes: Words and Pictures to Comfort, Inspire and Entertain* edited by Katherine Rundell, with contributions from over 100 children's authors and illustrators

## Fiction
*The Truth Pixie* by Matt Haig and Chris Mould

## Non-Fiction
*Counting on Katherine: How Katherine Johnson Put Astronauts on the Moon* by Helaine Becker and Dow Phumiruk
*Here We Are: Notes for Living on Planet Earth* by Oliver Jeffers
*How to Be Extraordinary* by Rashmi Sirdeshpande and Annabel Tempest
*Little Leaders: Bold Women in Black History* by Vashti Harrison
*Michael Rosen's Sad Book* by Michael Rosen and Quentin Blake
*My Skin, Your Skin: Let's Talk About Race, Racism and Empowerment* by Laura Henry-Allain MBE and Onyinye Iwu
*The Street Beneath My Feet* by Charlotte Guillain and Yuval Zommer
*Welcome to Our World: A Celebration of Children Everywhere!* by Moira Butterfield and Harriet Lynas

## Picture Books
*Ada Twist, Scientist* by Andrea Beaty and David Roberts
*All Are Welcome* by Alexandra Penfold and Suzanne Kaufman
*Amazing Grace* by Mary Hoffman and Caroline Binch
*Bloom* by Anne Booth and Robyn Owen Wilson
*The Boy, the Mole, the Fox and the Horse* by Charlie Mackesy
*Can Bears Ski?* by Raymond Antrobus and Polly Dunbar
*Can I Build Another Me?* by Shinsuke Yoshitake
*Colour and Me!* by Michaela Dias-Hayes
*The Colour Monster* by Anna Llenas
*The Comet* by Joe Todd-Stanton
*Coming to England: An Inspiring True Story Celebrating the Windrush Generation* by Floella Benjamin and Diane Ewen
*The Day the Crayons Quit* by Drew Daywalt and Oliver Jeffers
*The Day War Came* by Nicola Davies and Rebecca Cobb
*The Dot* by Peter H. Reynolds
*Elmer* by David McKee

*Eyes That Kiss in the Corners* by Joanna Ho and Dung Ho
*The Forgettery* by Rachel Ip and Laura Hughes
*The Girls* by Lauren Ace and Jenny Løvlie
*Happy in Our Skin* by Fran Manushkin and Lauren Tobia
*I Don't Like Books. Never. Ever. The End.* by Emma Perry and Sharon Davey
*The Invisible* by Tom Percival
*I Talk Like a River* by Jordan Scott and Sydney Smith
*It's a No-Money Day* by Kate Milner
*The Journey* by Francesca Sanna
*Julian Is a Mermaid* by Jessica Love
*Leaf* by Sandra Dieckmann
*Lights on Cotton Rock* by David Litchfield
*The Lion Inside* by Rachel Bright and Jim Field
*Little Glow* by Katie Sahota and Harry Woodgate
*Look Up!* by Nathan Bryon and Dapo Adeola
*The Lost Homework* by Richard O'Neill and Kirsti Beautyman
*Milo Imagines the World* by Matt de la Pena and Christian Robinson
*Mixed: An Inspiring Story About Colour* by Arree Chung
*My Hair* by Hannah Lee and Allen Fatimaharan
*Nen and the Lonely Fisherman* by Ian Eagleton and James Mayhew
*The Perfect Fit* by Naomi Jones and James Jones
*The Pirate Mums* by Jodie Lancet-Grant and Lydia Corry
*The Proudest Blue: A Story of Hijab and Family* by Ibtihaj Muhammad, S. K. Ali and Hatem Aly
*Rain Before Rainbows* by Smriti Halls and David Litchfield
*Ruby's Worry* by Tom Percival
*The Same But Different Too* by Karl Newson and Kate Hindley
*The Song for Everyone* by Lucy Morris
*Splash* by Claire Cashmore and Sharon Davey
*Sulwe* by Lupita Nyong'o and Vashti Harrison
*Through the Eyes of Me* by Jon Roberts and Hannah Rounding
*The Tin Forest* by Helen Ward and Wayne Anderson
*The Undefeated* by Kwame Alexander and Kadir Nelson
*Voices in the Park* by Anthony Browne
*We're All Wonders* by R. J. Palacio
*What Happened to You?* by James Catchpole and Karen George
*Where the Poppies Now Grow* by Hilary Robinson and Martin Impey
*Wisp: A Story of Hope* by Zana Fraillon and Grahame Baker Smith
*You Can* by Alexandra Strick and Steve Antony

## Poetry
*Being Me: Poems About Thoughts, Worries and Feelings* by Liz Brownlee, Matt Goodfellow, Laura Mucha and Victoria Jane Wheeler
*Courage in a Poem* by various authors

*I Am the Seed That Grew the Tree: A Nature Poem for Every Day of the Year* selected by Fiona Waters and illustrated by Frann Preston-Gannon
*The Lost Words* by Robert Macfarlane and Jackie Morris
*Poems Aloud* by Joseph Coelho and Daniel Gray-Barnett

**Wordless Picture Books**
*Door* by JiHyeon Lee
*Flotsam* by David Wiesner
*Here I Am* by Patti Kim and Sonia Sánchez
*Island* by Mark Janssen
*Journey* by Aaron Becker
*Wave* by Suzy Lee
*Window* by Jeannie Baker